we ♥ our city®

HOW A CHURCH IN THE COMMUNITY
BECAME THE COMMUNITY'S CHURCH

authorHOUSE®

AuthorHouse™
1663 Liberty Drive
Bloomington, IN 47403
www.authorhouse.com
Phone: 1 (800) 839-8640

Published by AuthorHouse 02/15/2018

ISBN: 978-1-5462-2190-6 (sc)
ISBN: 978-1-5462-2249-1 (e)

Print information available on the last page.

Any people depicted in stock imagery provided by Thinkstock are models,
and such images are being used for illustrative purposes only.
Certain stock imagery © Thinkstock.

This book is printed on acid-free paper.

Because of the dynamic nature of the Internet, any web addresses or
links contained in this book may have changed since publication and
may no longer be valid. The views expressed in this work are solely those
of the author and do not necessarily reflect the views of the publisher,
and the publisher hereby disclaims any responsibility for them.

Unless otherwise indicated, all scripture quotations are from The Holy Bible,
English Standard Version® (ESV®). Copyright ©2001 by Crossway Bibles, a
division of Good News Publishers. Used by permission. All rights reserved

Scripture quotations marked NIV are taken from the Holy Bible, New
International Version®. NIV®. Copyright © 1973, 1978, 1984 by International
Bible Society. Used by permission of Zondervan. All rights reserved. [Biblica]

Contents

Contents

Foreword

This book is the story of a journey of a small handful of people called church planters who set out to make a difference in "small town America" not really knowing what it would look like or how to get there, yet determined to build a church that would have an impact beyond the predictable cycles of weekend church activity. Our community, The Father's House, is currently 21 years into this journey and it's been a great ride so far and only picking up pace. The big "ah ha" moment for me, and the reason I believe you should read this book, was the revelation of how simply serving and loving the city that God had set us down in would take on a life of its own, it would grow, radically multiply, open doors, bring resources, reach thousands and be a continual life-flow of fresh vision, favor and passion for our church. I'm convinced one of the missing elements in many churches across our nation is this simple, yet profound platform that is built when we partner with our city leaders and organizations by serving the needs of the broken and under resourced with no other agenda than to love and serve the people that are in great need. Kinda like Jesus. We all know it's Biblical, we know we should be doing something about the glaring needs around us and every self-respecting, bible-based church is having a go at feeding some hungry people and helping some widows. Where this book and our journey may help you is to show you how to implement a city impact vision and strategy that will make your local church an unavoidable force in your community.

This book is written in three parts. Part I, the first 5 chapters, are written by Pastor Raymond. Raymond and Kim Beaty are our Community Outreach pastors. Pastor Raymond is also our Prison Campus Pastor, one of our teaching team and a busy City activist, all while overseeing, what is now, a large organization that feeds over 25,000 people every month in 3 counties. (more details on the scope of the ministry in the coming chapters). All that to say, we call Raymond "the Godfather of Compassion" & "the Mafia Boss of Benevolence". In the early chapters, you will find some incredible research, hard data and answers to questions that should be ask by every pastor and leadership team.

Then in Part II, I will give you some practical applications, lead pastor perspectives and personal challenges in this journey. I truly believe God has given us a template, a strategy and a clear roadmap that will work in every community (with necessary modifications required) that will produce similar results and bring our churches to the forefront of our cities and in the bullseye of New Testament mandates.

Who is this book for? Primarily this is written to lead pastors and church planters. I believe the keys to the cities we live in are entrusted to the pastors that God appoints to reach those cities. We simply need to discover those keys, pick them up and use them for God's glory. This book is also written for leadership teams and anyone who wants to make an impact for eternity by loving their city in a tangible way.

Part III of this book is a 'show and tell' of how we are practically loving our city. The goal is to give you some nuts and bolts, some ideas to consider and strategies that can be implemented incrementally. As a lead pastor, church planter and kingdom guy, it's always been my deep desire to be a part of a church that people could not easily ignore or live in proximity to, while never knowing we existed. By God's grace and our journey of loving our city, we are living that dream in these great days of God's favor. My prayer is this book, and our years of building, can help to serve other leaders and churches to get a bigger vision for their community, get busy serving them and go farther faster for the Glory of God.

Dave Patterson
Lead Pastor
The Father's House

Preface

The subtitle of this book is an actual quote from one of our city council members. I was asked to make a presentation to the city council one evening on all the projects we, as a church, had partnered with the city on to provide social services to our community. One of the reasons for the report was to introduce the newest partnership, in which we as a church would become the city's official graffiti abatement team. After everyone on the city council took an opportunity to thank our church for the services we were providing to the community, one of them said, "Because of all that The Father's House is doing in our community, the city is a better place to live. This is how a church in the community became the community's church."

The partnership between the church and the city was years in the making. There is a fair amount of distrust on both sides of the policies, protocols, and practices of each side. After years of working on justice-related issues I often spent much of my time being a liaison between faith-based, local, city, county, state, and federal organizations. The delicate, often exhausting dance between organizations is created by the inflexibility of the policies, protocols, and practices of the separate entities. The justice for those who need relief routinely becomes a journey into a maze that results from all the different organizations created to secure justice. Since every organization has its own policies, protocols, and procedures that never seem to connect with other organizations, people who are in need of justice get lost in the maze. This is where it gets personal for me. Often the worst offender of too many policies, protocols, and procedures, and nonparticipation with other organizations, is the church, and I say this as a pastor who loves the church that Christ died for and that I have faithfully served for over thirty years.

When the "We Love Our City," weloveourcity. org, community outreaches began at our church, we were serving several hundred underresourced people in different ways. After years of learning how to partner with different organizations, we now feed over twenty-five thousand people every month at our food banks in three different cities. Each one of these cities has a population of over one hundred thousand people. On a weekly basis we provide fresh produce to five underserved elementary schools in three cities with a total student population of over five thousand. We work in twenty-five different high-risk neighborhoods representing over ninety blocks on a weekly basis in five different cities. Not included in the twenty-five thousand people we feed at our three food banks are the people we feed every Saturday in five different cities of our "Adopt a Block" program. Over ninety blocks receive free food every Saturday, and I don't even know how many thousands that is because they do not sign government forms for the donated food, and we don't count; we just serve. We serve as the official graffiti abatement team for two cities and the Napa Valley, manage a community center that provides a free afterschool program and summer program in one of our at-risk neighborhoods. We have free mobile medical clinics and free bookmobiles that travel to those in need of these services. We recently converted what was known at city hall as the "Ghetto Trail" into a one-acre community garden in the most violent area of the city. We have a mobile hair salon, a mobile dental clinic, and a mobile vision clinic. We supply birthday cakes and free tennis shoes to every child under the age of thirteen in all ninety of our blocks and provide grocery gift cards to the homeless who come and work at our food banks.

In all of these cities, our projects happened in partnership with federal, state, county, and city organizations and in cooperation with other programs that churches typically will not include or support as part of their community outreach based on the overused and often misused phrase "separation between church and state." While the First Amendment to the Constitution does provide some protection for churches from government, it was never meant to prohibit partnerships with government. For many churches, their form of social justice is so clearly designed around the same inflexible policies, protocols, and practices that governments have been accused of using, that create a cycle of poverty. This means that churches often trap people in need in the same kind of bureaucratic maze and deny true justice for those who need it most. It has been my experience that many churches seem unwilling to accept help or to partner with organizations that don't share their policies, protocols, or procedures, which is behavior resembling the kind of religious rigidity that Jesus often spoke against. It makes the church that Jesus died for look sectarian, elitist, and uncooperative, all the while claiming to be "in the world but not of the world."

Of course, there is plenty of finger-pointing we can do at other organizations as well. We have all heard the stories of government waste and systemic abuse of social programs. Programs that by design were targeted to assist those in need but are often overadministrated or underadministrated to the point of resources being squandered or mismanaged in such a way that those who need it don't receive it. From the federal level down to local municipalities, there is the need to reevaluate the programs, their target demographic, and the management systems in place. It shows up in this <u>recent report</u> from the Cato Institute, which argues that the federal government spends $668 billion per year on 126 different welfare programs (spending by state and local governments pushes that figure up to $1 trillion per year). The <u>Government Accountability Office</u> (GAO) released a report claiming to have identified $48 billion in what is termed as "improper payments." That's nearly 10 percent of the $500 billion in outlays for that year. However, others, including past US Attorney General Eric Holder, <u>suggest that</u> there is an estimated $60 to $90 billion in Medicare fraud and a similar amount for Medicaid. The list goes on.

But what if the government didn't have to spend so much money doing what the church was supposed to be doing in the first place? What if there was a way for all the interested parties to come together and each one do what that organization does well without the partisan political rhetoric and hypocritical holy rants about policy, protocols, procedures, or religious rancor? What if the church in your city could really be a Matthew 5:14 church: "You are the light of the world. A city built on a hill cannot be hidden." What if your church in your community became the community's church?

Raymond Beaty
Community Outreach Pastor
The Father's House

ENDORSEMENTS

I couldn't put this book down, neither will you! As the chief of Police of Vacaville California, I see every day the needs of our community, the challenges of the poor and homelessness, and everyone trying to do their part in "giving back" and striving to help people in need. As a leader in government, I draw stakeholders together, but it requires everyone to bring resources to the table, leverage effective strategies, and collaborate in order to be effective in improving life conditions. I have personally witnessed the poverty of Haiti, and struggle with the challenges of impoverished neighborhoods even in my own community, whether feeding the hungry or clothing the poor. I have seen many individuals and organizations focus on giving and serving, but Dave Patterson and Raymond Beaty and their vision behind "We Love Our City" stands above the rest.

Raymond Beaty is a straight forward "get it done" pastor and community leader who knows how to get results. His strategies entrenched in The Fathers House church outreach ministry known as "We Love Our City" can be seen on his office wall like a mural, a matrix of programs, networks and systems, all interlinked in order to organize and deliver coordinated services that every community needs. It's impressive, and effective.

Dave and Raymond share their views on the pursuit for justice, and how the church measures up against the government. You may be surprised by what is revealed in this book, but there is no doubt if you feel called to help others, you just might have a personal revelation that will be life changing. They will challenge you to encounter people where they live, have compassion for them in the moment, and care for the need they are experiencing. I urge you to listen up, suspend your personal assumptions, and think about what it means to care for people in need, not just their needs.

If you are involved in serving or desire to help others, whether through your local church or other faith-based or non-profit organization, this book is a must read. Understanding the role of the church in meeting the needs of your community is paramount if you want be effective. Maybe you are actively responsible for outreach programs or simply giving your time to help others, it is crucial that you know what to do, how to do it effectively, why it is necessary, and who is really responsible. We Love Our City walks you through these issues as they share real world experiences and life lessons, all in order to equip and prepare your mind and your heart.

This provocative book will have you engaged and will compel you to rethink roles of the church, government, and elected officials. It will also cause you to reevaluate your purpose while serving, and what is required when you encounter people in need. We Love Our City establishes a bold perspective on service, historical lessons from Scripture, and personal captivating stories that will provide insight into controversial issues at the center of the Church and the soul of Its followers. We Love Our City will take you on a field trip of your own and will prepare your heart for a journey that you were made for.

John Carli
Chief of Police
Vacaville, California

Separation of church and state is a fundamental rule of the government. As a City Planner and a City Manager- with over 30 years of local government experience- there were points of friction with faith-based organizations. This was because most faith-based groups have tight budgets and use a lot of volunteers to get things done. But the government has to treat everyone the same- the rules are the rules. Raymond's experience as a pastor confirms the lack of trust and the conflicts between church and state. This conflict exists in most communities, as religion and government just don't mix.

The setting for We love Our City is Vacaville, California, at a difficult time during the Great Recession. A popular growing church, The Father's House or TFH, was (and still is) doing great things in the community. The Great Recession caused cities across the nation to cut millions from their budgets. Vacaville was no exception. We were forced to implement difficult- often heart wrenching- program cuts. At the same time, there was a very messy fight going on between the State leaders and the cities. We were all fighting to keep our funding sources and it became the perfect storm. Governor Brown lead the charge to strip away the popular financial tool called Redevelopment. While folks have varying opinions on the topic, properly used redevelopment agencies did great and wonderful things. Which was the case in Vacaville.

One Redevelopment funded program that was cut: graffiti abatement. Soon after, Vacaville started to look pretty bad. Then, Raymond shows up and he offers up his crew of volunteers to provide this service. Given the circumstances, we couldn't turn him down. We all took a risk in creating what could have been seen as taboo- a church/state relationship! We found that Raymond and his team did it better- and faster- than the City had. Vacaville looked great. Soon after, We Love Our City was born as a separate non-profit organization from TFH. This also solved a lot of other potentially sticky problems.

Today, We Love Our City is offering after school programs in a former Boys and Girls Club Center, and various other services in an old Greyhound Bus Station- both city owned facilities. All the services are helping at risk residents, especially the homeless, and the community at large. The relationship was a success, which helped Raymond expand beyond Vacaville.

Many people have misconceptions about the under sourced members of our community- myself included. The effects of the homelessness, gangs, crime, and drugs continue to be a huge struggle. It is easy to make assumptions about those who are "the problem" and that "they" have to change to make it better. Raymond's writings give us a new window of understanding and how our misconceptions create barriers to solving problems. In the end, our views and assumptions need to be left at the door. And, we have to be willing to change some of the rules of the game.

We love Our City gives you insight as to the under sourced population's reality. Creating healthy and stable environments for everyone is the cornerstone of creating a better community, which starts with just being nice to each other.

Laura Kuhn
City Manager (Retired)
City of Vacaville

PART I

PART I

Congress or Church

The first missing piece to our pursuit of justice is answering this question: Whose responsibility is it to provide justice? While Congress would bristle at the comparison that they are functioning as a church, and the church would revolt at the comparison that they should be functioning as a Congress, the comparisons are undeniable. Here is a short civics lesson for you. It all began with the cry, "no taxation without representation." People want to be heard, respected, and represented fairly. When it became obvious that people in the New World were not going to be heard, respected, or represented fairly, they decided to take matters into their own hands. After mixing some tea with some seawater, a uniquely American drink was created that initiated the "justice for just us" sentiment. And after complete commitment of our resources, our will, and our lives to that pursuit, we began a country with a system of government that provided for its citizens to be heard, respected, and represented fairly. Even with all of its shortcomings and ineffectiveness, Congress is still the world's best example of a democracy as a place where people are provided the opportunity to participate in the protection and provision of their lives and the lives of others by electing a representative government that convenes as a congress to provide liberty and justice for all.

It sounds like something the church should be doing. In fact, the pursuit of fairness and justice in our personal faith pursuit is as American as our Boston seawater tea. Men and women came to the free world with the dream of serving God in a way that gave them a choice. It seemed an injustice to compel people to believe a certain way and then have them punished or killed if they did not conform. Therefore, the pursuit of religious freedom as a matter of justice is a driving force of the American church. But for some reason, somewhere along the way, the church forgot that justice was to extend beyond personal choice of faith to include personal responsibility and to ensure justice for others. Our fledgling country, and her new government, was born out of the justice of personal freedoms and was quick to adapt to and has continued the process of ensuring justice for all groups. The church, however, seems to have chosen to enjoy the justice of her freedom without the same responsibility of ensuring justice for others. Unfortunately there is proof. According to the most recent census, the United States has over 325 million people. Those 325 million people are represented by one hundred United States senators and 435 United States representatives. On a national level, 535 people are responsible for setting standards, writing legislation, budgeting, and managing the collective will of the people. And regardless of what you think about their performance, or their ability to work together, here is what they are doing for the demographic of people who are, as Christians would say, "the least of these."

In a 2013 Center on Budget and Policy Priorities outline of how federally collected taxes were used to finance public services, it was found that about 12 percent of the federal budget in 2013, or $398 billion, supported safety net programs that provided aid (other than health insurance or Social Security benefits) to individuals and families facing hardship. These programs include the refundable portions of the Earned Income Tax Credit and Child Tax Credit, which assist low- and moderate-income working families through the tax code programs that provide cash payments to eligible individuals or households, including Supplemental Security Income for the elderly or disabled poor and unemployment insurance; various forms of in-kind assistance for low-income families and individuals, including SNAP (food stamps), school meals, low-income housing assistance, child-care assistance, and assistance in meeting home energy bills; and various other programs such as those that aid abused and neglected children. These programs keep millions of people out of poverty each year. A CBPP analysis shows that government safety net programs kept some forty-one million people out of poverty in calendar year 2012. Without any government income assistance, either from safety net programs or other income supports such as Social Security, the poverty rate would have been 29.1 percent in 2012, nearly double the actual 16 percent.

Now that we know the scope of what the government is doing to provide aid to those in need, let's take a look at what the church is doing. Before you look at the numbers, I understand that the argument can be made that the government has access to more money, or you may argue that churches are so autonomous that it cannot really be known how much they are giving. Clearly the government is more resourced through the force of law than the church is by her gentle reminders, but there is very accurate information as to the percentages and amounts that churches give to "social programs," or better known in church circles as benevolence to "the least of these."

The Evangelical Christian Credit Union, with over $1,921,357,504 total assets under management, was asked about its budget allocations based on thirty-two budget line-items and five expense categories. Participating churches were also asked which topics would be of interest to them for future ECCU resources. Although budget allocations differ significantly when compared to a Christianity Today International survey, on average, they remain consistent across churches of varying sizes. In a line by line budget breakdown including allocations for things such as pastoral salaries, office supplies, and facility maintenance, the average expense participating churches recorded annually for benevolence was only 1 percent.

You do the math. Congress 12 percent, church 1 percent. Or stated in one of those sixth-grade math word problems, if one group that didn't have the moral responsibility to care for poor people gave 12 percent of its budget to programs designed to aid poor people, and one group that did have the moral responsibility to take care of poor people gave 1 percent of its budget to programs designed to aid poor people, which group has actually taken moral responsibility (the key to the answer is to work the problem from the perspective of a poor person). Both entities have recorded documents available to them to help them set the percentages. Congress works from a mandate of the people and the values they reflect and passes bills to enact the percentages. The church has a mandate from the creator of the people and the values He reflects, and clearly recorded those values to enact the percentages. I never did enjoy math, but a math formula where Congress does a better job of reflecting values and percentages than the church, well … now I really don't like math.

Before it all ends up sounding like some political, philosophical, theological rant by an angry blogger somewhere, let's close this chapter with the truth. When does God start talking about justice? In the beginning. From Genesis to the New Testament, it is the cry of His heart. I am going to focus primarily on what He says about justice in the book of Proverbs. Let's start with Proverbs 21:3: "to do righteousness and justice is desired more than sacrifice" (NASB). It really doesn't get any clearer than that. You can empty out your pockets, give all you want, sacrificially give of your time, and publicly make declarations of how you want the world to change, but God says you better do something. Do righteousness and justice. And what is really fascinating here is He is not talking about two different topics. Righteousness over here and justice over here. The same words for righteousness and justice are used in Hebrew and Greek. The Hebrew word and its variants mean both righteousness and justice; the same is true for the Greek word. They are used interchangeably. The link is found in the meaning of justice, which is to act rightly. It is the character of God to act rightly, to do justice. Psalm 11:7 says, "the Lord is righteous he loves justice." Psalm 33:5 says, "The Lord loves righteousness and justice." It is rooted in the character of God. He even sits on a throne, according to Psalm 89, that has as its foundation righteousness and justice.

All through Proverbs, He talks about how He hates false weights and double standards, dishonest scales, and bribes. If it is a tangible example of justice, it must be right, and if it is right, you must do it—it is justice.

All of this flows out of the character of God; it is His nature to do justice. There is no other place more important to Him to do justice than with and for the people who need justice. It is the character and heart of God to be unimpressed with your sacrifice and your fasting and to be moved with your compassion for the hungry, homeless, oppressed, abused, and those held captive. Social justice has always been His heart (Isaiah 58). Listen, when the creator of the universe starts talking about His heart for social justice in the beginning of the universe to every prophet, priest, and people from the Old Testament and continues to talk about it on through the New Testament, it is important. When important people say important things we should listen, or it can be very painful. Here is a personal example of not listening to instructions from an important person, and the pain it creates.

A few years ago I joined a team of climbers to be a part of a winter expedition on Mount Rainier. The goal was to summit this fourteen-thousand-foot peak in the worst winter conditions possible as training to continue on and climb Mount McKinley. The leader of the expedition was Jim Whittaker, the first American to ever climb Mount Everest. I made sure I took my hero picture with him because I was so proud to be climbing with this important legend in the world of climbing. The expedition started by loading all the gear needed for a two-week trip on a sled that each climber would pull up the mountain. Each sled weighed about one hundred pounds, and in the early part of the climb there were lots of uphills and downhills as we made our way to the ridge that we would be climbing to the summit. I began to think as the first few days passed that on the downhill portion of the trip, it didn't make any sense to use the method the world class climber had taught us for declines, and I had a much better idea. His procedure sounded like so much work. Why do I want to let the trailing rope down slowly over a decline when I can just shove it over the edge, and go get it after it stops? I was going to show this mountaineer who had reached the summit of the tallest mountains on every continent in the world a new way to release a one-hundred-pound sled down a decline. I was even going to call it the "Beaty belay." So ... I line it up, and I shove it over the edge; about the time I shove it, I remember I am still tied to it … It is like a cartoon happening in slow motion. I (and everyone else) saw what was going to happen but couldn't do anything about it. When a one-hundred-pound sled reaches the end of a fifteen-foot rope going downhill, there is nothing but pain.

I really believe that is what the church has done with social justice. I believe we have piled all the difficult, seemingly unsolvable ugliness and pain of social issues onto a sled, covered it up with good intentions, and shoved it over the edge. The church is watching from a distance. But I promise you, the end of the rope is coming, and if we do not do justice, not only will the pain continue for others, but we are going to feel the sudden snap at the end of the rope that results in chaos that comes from a world with no justice. There is a rope of justice that God tied to your heart from His heart. There is no untying it.

Here is one of the reasons I think the church watches from a distance: government social programs. That's right I put it in writing, and I am going to take it further. Let's talk about government social programs. This is where you think you are going to find out what my political affiliation is when I start talking about government social programs. You think you are going to find out whether I am a Republican, Democrat, Independent, Libertarian, Green Party, Tea Party, let's have a party, or who invited you to my party. What you are really going to find out is what God says about government social programs. The word of the Lord on government social programs is that it never was the government's responsibility to take care of the widows and orphans—it is the church's responsibility; it never was the government's responsibility to free those in slavery—it is the church's responsibility; it never was the government's responsibility to house the homeless—it is the church's responsibility; it never was the government's responsibility to feed the hungry—it is the church's responsibility; it never was the government's responsibility to make sure people have clothes—it is the church's responsibility; it never was the government's responsibility to defend the weak and oppressed—it is the church's responsibility. Congress or church? Come on, church! The first missing piece in our pursuit of justice is answering this question: Whose responsibility is it to provide justice? I believe one of the beliefs that keeps the church on the sideline while Congress tries to fill the gap is an insidious unspoken belief that poor people are dumb people, so why try. Poor people are not dumb people!

Poor People Are Not Dumb People

Here is the second missing piece to our pursuit of justice. Poor people are not dumb people. This is not so much an attempt on my part to hold the general public responsible for a widely held misconception as it is an embarrassing admission on my part. In the last four years, our programs that provide opportunities to the underresourced have grown exponentially. As a result of the growth of the programs, I have had the pleasure of meeting thousands of underresourced people who have taught me more about courage, dignity, resilience, and humanity than any other experience in my life. As I shake hands and listen to stories of those standing in our food lines or families living in difficult parts of town or the children we help with their homework in our after-school programs, there is a determination in their voices to be more than they have been provided the opportunity to be. I know the common misconception is if you stand in line for handouts or can't seem to raise your standard of living beyond the difficult parts of town you live in or don't excel in school, it has to be your fault at many levels. These people didn't try hard enough or work hard enough or study hard enough to change their circumstances. So they must be either lazy or dumb or both. I know dumb is not the politically correct word for individuals who have limited capacity, but that is just the point. Underresourced people do not have limited capacity; they have limited opportunities. And while you see just enough of the underresourced demographic not trying or conclude by their actions that they are not thinking, it seems to justify the misconception. It is, both in my personal experience and by the numbers, a vindictive misconception. In a recently released book entitled *Hand to Mouth*, Linda Tirado writes about the truth about being poor in a wealthy world. As a part of the working poor, she wrote in an attempt to educate people that poor people are in fact not dumb people. Critics were skeptical about her claims until they had done enough research to understand she was describing nearly a third of the American population. When she was asked why she thinks people were so skeptical, she answered with fierce conviction: "Because it's easier to think poor people really are all stupid. It's easier to think we can't look like you, to think downward mobility doesn't exist, only upward." Her book challenges a collective blindness to a nation's grim economic truths. "We have homeless PhDs, middle-class people on food stamps and 25% of all active duty military accessing food banks on a regular basis. Poverty is a reality to more people than we're willing to admit." There is, she believes, a real fear of poverty in America, a country that clings to the notion that hard work is all you need to succeed. "I haven't had it worse than anyone else," she writes. "This is just what life is for roughly one third of Americans."

Poor parents are easily some of the most vilified individuals. Something about not being flush with cash to dote on your children automatically makes you the absolute dumbest, laziest, and most inept parent, who, according to many comments I've read over the years, deserves to have your children taken away—like foster care is some magical, plush dreamland where kiddies are welcomed inside with hugs and freshly baked cookies. But a study on the vicious cycle of poverty demonstrates that being under financial duress actually just makes you think differently. And not all that well. MSNBC reports that "being poor affects your ability to think" and that being under "severe" financial stress doesn't give you the capability—or "mental bandwidth"— to make stellar choices. Apparently, being strapped for cash takes up so much mental energy that poor decisions follow. People use the phrase, "it is like _____ on crack." Fill in the blank with whatever you want. People use it because crack became such an epidemic in our society beginning in the '80s, and its impact and consequences were so severe that people felt it was was a great way to explain anything that was tragic, intense, severe, or of epidemic proportions. It's now well over two decades since the worst of the epidemic, and many of the medical consequences were determined not to be as severe as initially reported. One of the common misconceptions was the medical consequences for "crack babies." According to a twenty-four-year study of these so-called "crack babies," prenatal use of crack cocaine had little to no effect on kids directly. That in and of itself is surprising, but there's even more: while performing this study, researchers discovered something. While crack might not cause adverse issues directly, parenting a child without money certainly does. In the late 1980s, Dr. Hallam Hurt, the chair of the neonatology department at Philadelphia's Albert Einstein Medical Center, started following 224 full- or near-full-term babies born to crack addicted mothers. Over the years, the study found that on average the IQs of the "crack babies'" were on the same level as the control group of noncrack babies, and they also had comparable outcomes in emotional and educational developments. Basically, there were *no* major differences. What they *did* find was that poverty itself caused a lot of serious issues for children. Now, on one hand, poverty often goes hand in hand with drug use, but this isn't always the case, and the two are far from exclusive to each other. Hurt's study showed that kids who are raised in poverty tended to have lower IQs, less school readiness, and more anxiety, depression, and cognitive functioning problems than kids who have more means. This was true regardless of whether their mothers were addicted to crack. Hurt believes that the issue here is the environments in which these children are raised. The vast majority of them personally witness violence and crime well before they are eighteen. According to Hurt: "Those children who reported a high exposure to violence were likelier to show signs of depression and anxiety and to have lower self-esteem." She went on to say, "Given what we learned, we are invested in better understanding the effects of poverty. How can early effects be detected? Which developing systems are affected? And most important, how can findings inform interventions for our children?" You can't argue that the crack epidemic of the 1980s wasn't historic or life-changing for the millions of people it affected. Everywhere you turned there was another TV show or newspaper article claiming that kids born to addicts would face issues such as birth defects, severe emotional issues, and reduced learning abilities. But why is it easier for us, as a society, to blame the "crack-addicted welfare queen" rather than the economic inequities that contributed to the problem in the first place? We now know that it's not just the drugs, but the lack of resources, education, food, and other means that hurts kids. It almost makes you want to say that being poor is more dangerous than crack.

Another reason poor people are often believed to be dumb people is the type of food they eat, which often leads to weight or health problems. If you are not poor, you are more prone to say something like, "No wonder they are fat with all the fast food and fried food they eat." Shockingly, when you're buying food based entirely on 1) how long it keeps and 2) how cheap it is, you wind up with food that is bad and bad for you. Underresourced families who rely on SNAP, or the Supplemental Nutrition Assistance Program, a.k.a. "food stamps" know that the first of each month is grocery day. These days, food stamps come in the form of an ATM-type card that gets reloaded with "food only" money on the first of every month. Often when the food money arrives, families will purchase an entire month's worth of groceries to be stored.

When this is done, food that will not spoil must be purchased, which means these families can forget about fresh produce or fresh baked goods or fresh anything for that matter. Canned fruit and vegetables could be split between multiple people for half the cost of fresh ones, and at the end you have the extra surprise of pure, liquefied sugar to push you into full-blown diabetes. What isn't canned is frozen. Think TV dinners, pizzas, chicken nuggets, anything that can be frozen forever and doesn't require a lot of preparation. Of course, by week two, whatever is left is freezer burned, and with the distinct taste of canned food, poor people grow to think that this is the way food is supposed to taste. When and if fresh fruits and vegetables are ever introduced into their diet, often they are rejected. Think about green beans, for instance; there is a considerable difference in texture and taste between the canned vs. the fresh version. Another example is the difference between boxed and homemade macaroni and cheese. I'm sure you can think of more; the list goes on and on. Processed food choices have been eaten for so long that they are often preferred to the fresh version. Have you ever heard someone point out, or even thought to yourself, that many people in underresourced areas do not look hungry based on their size or shape? But what you absolutely must remember is that the reason many of them have weight problems is because the majority of everything they consume is dirt-cheap, processed garbage. Grab a frozen dinner and look at the nutritional information. The calories, sodium, and sugar content are high, and the ingredients are questionable.

Fresh food is expensive. It doesn't stay fresh

long, requiring multiple trips to the grocery store per month, and this just isn't something most underresourced people can do. All those money-saving frozen meals, high in salt and fat, are major contributing factors to the expanding bodies of the people who simply can't afford anything else. It is discouraging for underresourced parents to know that they are living off of food they know isn't good for them or their children. As if being poor didn't already present enough to worry about, your personal battles become punch lines and topics for judgment.

For example, Ted Nugent, famous rocker and outspoken critic of the poor, often publicly demonizes those in poverty. He describes them as "stupid" and having "no one to blame but themselves," while attacking their access to "luxuries" such as "air-conditioning" and "clean water." Nugent complains that "America's so-called *poor* live a life far better than do real poor people around the world and have luxuries they can only dream of." He suggests cutting "social welfare programs" as punishment for "poor decisions." Nugent calls for disenfranchising those who don't pay federal income taxes and taking away the voting rights of the working poor and retirees. While his stated views on the underresourced do seem to have them in a stranglehold, I am more concerned about how these views seem to be either stated or lived by the general public, more specifically, the church. It is astounding how intelligent people can come to a conclusion that those around them who are less fortunate, less resourced, and have less opportunity are somehow less intelligent than they are. I have to admit that I received quite an education myself in these past few years of being immersed in a demographic that has very few resources or opportunities.

While I don't believe I ever thought that poor people are dumb people, I have embarrassed and astounded myself with some of my assumptions that proved to be biased in that direction after conversations with people who stand in our food lines every day. Of the dozens of ways I have caught myself in my own unspoken bias, the one that still makes me shake my head in disbelief at how ignorant I was, is about a man named Anthony (not his real name). Anthony is in his midthirties, works construction when he can find work, is married, and has two daughters. He comes to our food bank every day that he is not working, and his wife comes when he has work. He's a hard-working guy doing the best he can in a slow California economy. One day he asked me if I knew of any hotel rooms he could rent by the month because the one he was at was increasing from $800 a month to $1,000 a month. Now if you are as biased as I was, you are immediately thinking, "That is dumb; he could rent an apartment for that amount of money." And

I immediately began to give him a lesson on finance and "smarter" choices on his living arrangements. He patiently listened until I was finished and said, "Here is the problem with your advice: the neighborhoods that I can find an apartment for that price are the neighborhoods I intentionally moved out of." He said, "I grew up in those neighborhoods, did my first drug deal, joined my first gang, got arrested for the first time in those neighborhoods. The schools are bad, the neighborhood is dangerous, and the relationships are destructive." He began to help me understand that the reason he lived in a motel on the other side of town was because the schools were great, the neighborhood was safe, and there were parks and swimming pools and activities his wife and his girls could walk to. He had made a very logical, critical-thinking, informed, deliberate decision to do the best thing for his family. He was smart; I was dumb. Please remember the second missing piece to our pursuit of justice is that poor people are not dumb people. Because we so often treat poor people like dumb people, we offer them care, not compassion, which leads us to the next missing piece.

Not Care, Compassion

Here is the third missing piece to our pursuit of justice: not care, compassion. For God's sake, just be nice. It really is that simple. If you are not a religious person or don't believe in any higher power or cosmic force, or have any philosophical or scientific approach to life, it is still not hard to just be nice for nice sake. If you are a religious person or find yourself a follower of a great leader in times past, I am sure they would want you to just be nice. If you believe in God as I do, I know for a fact he wants you to be nice and not just for the sake of being nice but for His sake as well. If you are going to profess to be a follower of God, then for God's sake, the sake of His name, His nature, His desire to love everyone, you can start to show people his love by just being nice, which helps explain the title of this chapter. There is an enormous difference between offering care to someone instead of compassion.

The world is full of people who out of obligation

will offer some guilt-generated response to meet a need to offer the care that might be needed without offering the compassion that should motivate it. We would rather be efficient as opposed to being compassionate because compassion seems to take so much more effort. We would prefer to meet the need and move on, offering care but not compassion. Compassion doesn't even seem to register on the scale of our emotions when it comes to the poor. Nice seems to be as good as it gets but rarely is offered because offering care is easier and quicker. Sympathy, empathy, compassion, and caring are connected concepts, with different definitions. These concepts require more specific exploration in order to fully understand and apply them.

There are various and rather vague characterizations of sympathy. As defined, sympathy generally centers on an emotional state or feeling. It manifests in most people as pity or sorrow for another. The simplest definition is "the agreement in feeling." Empathy, by contrast, is characterized by identification *and* understanding. Empathy speaks to identifying with and experiencing the feelings, thoughts, and/or attitudes of another. Furthermore, compassion itself is the awareness of suffering in another and the desire to act in order to relieve it, meaning that compassion is best understood as an action. Imagine a world where everyone lived in an awareness of other people's suffering and acted in order to relieve it. There's a word for it. It's called justice, and it is "just us" who can bring it, but it must be driven by compassion, not care.

By definition, compassion is the feeling of deep sympathy and sorrow that arises for another who is stricken by misfortune, accompanied by the strong desire to alleviate the suffering. Compassion is not the same as sympathy or empathy because it includes action. There are cynics who dismiss compassion as touchy-feely and irrational, but scientists have actually started to map the biology of compassion. The science of compassion shows that when people feel compassion, their heart rate slows down, they secrete oxytocin—the "love hormone" associated with bonding, and regions of the brain that are linked to empathy, providing care, and feelings of pleasure ignite.

There are even university-level compassion training programs at multiple Ivy League schools guiding students how to expand compassion in themselves and others. The teachings within these types of programs provide a foundation of real-life applications that everyone is capable of implementing. To start, look for commonalities. Trying to see yourself as similar to others can increase your capacity for compassion. Next, calm your inner worry. See if you can keep your mind from responding with fear regarding someone else's pain; this can biologically inhibit the ability to enable compassion. Then, encourage cooperation over competition. Much of this will come from the words you speak to and about others. Follow with training yourself to see people as individuals. You will find a series of statistics in this book. While data is an important component in understanding hunger in our country, I promise you that is not what drives our outreaches, but the individual faces and stories of people we encounter each day. Remember not to play the blame game. Blaming others for their circumstances will make you feel less tenderness and concern toward them. Be empowered by your capability to make a difference and savor how good it feels to be compassionate. Set an example for the children around you by modeling kindness. Compassion is contagious, and this cultivation will manifest positively in the next generation. Lastly and oh so importantly, curb inequality. Do not ever allow yourself to feel a greater sense of status over another. This will interfere with your ability to practice true compassion.

I know all this sounds very academic, analytical, and in many ways obvious. But if you take a look at the way we treat each other, it doesn't really seem that anybody is really doing it. You can make a great case from all the nonprofit charitable work that goes on in the world. You can list the NGOs of the world and all of the care that is being provided through government agencies, privately funded groups, and good people all over the world just try trying to help others. I would argue that one of the reasons we never seem to make any progress in stemming the tide of the relentless need for care in the world is because we spend so much of our time and money caring for the need without caring about the people. As a pastor, I often default to biblical examples of this principle. Obviously Jesus went around caring for the needs of people, offering care whenever it was needed, but it was always from the compassion he had for people not just caring for the need. While there are parallel accounts in the gospel of the same story, I will just focus on Matthew for some examples. In Matthew 9, Jesus shows us that it is not about care; it is about compassion. In Matthew 9, Jesus heals a crippled man, a lady who had been sick for twelve years, a little girl who everyone thought was dead, two blind men, and a man who could not talk! Toward the end of the chapter, it says He goes to towns and villages healing every kind of disease and sickness! That is just chapter 9, and those stories are not even the most important part of the chapter. The last three verses hold the key as to why He healed people. It says He had compassion for them. He didn't heal because He could heal (care); He healed because He had to heal (compassion). He was so emotionally overtaken by the condition that He found these people in; He felt so personally and intimately the pain of their loss and sickness that He had to do something. This is not the only passage you will find Jesus doing miraculous things for people not just by His power over people but out of His heart for people. Take some time and read Matthew 14 and 15, Mark 6, 8, and 9, Luke 7, 10, and 15, and the list goes on and on demonstrating the heart of God when it comes to caring for people. Caring is a by-product of compassion; caring has to be driven by the same deep emotional, intimate, love of people and the sharing of their pain that Jesus had before you can provide them with the care they need. The third missing piece to our pursuit of justice is not care; it is compassion. Just meeting someone's needs without compassion not only misses the heart of God, but it also has a personal consequence. It makes you oblivious, even ignorant, to the most basic of people's needs, resulting in the fourth missing piece to our pursuit of justice, which is that people are hungry because you are ignorant.

People Are Hungry Because You Are Ignorant

Here is the fourth missing piece to our pursuit of justice: people are hungry, and what you thought you knew may not actually be the truth. *Don't be ignorant of the facts.* Did you know that one in every four *active-duty service personnel* goes to a food bank because they don't have enough food to make it until the end of the month? If learning that 25 percent of active-duty service members and their families suffer from food insecurity alarms you, as it should, this chapter will replace what you thought you knew about hunger in America with an informed foundation based on a summary of a comprehensive study by Feeding America. After all, we do not want you to be ignorant. Feeding America is a nonprofit leading the nation in the fight against hunger. The complete report, titled "Hunger in America," is a series of studies that takes place every four years. The study's purpose is to provide demographic profiles of those seeking food assistance through the Feeding America network in order to better serve the affected population. It is the largest study in America to provide this type of information. Through interviews with more than sixty thousand clients and thirty-two thousand partner agencies, the data collected helps to direct programs and solutions aimed at improving food security, increasing public awareness, and encouraging policy development for addressing hunger in the United States. Food security refers to the household-level economic and social condition of reliable access to an adequate amount of food for an active, healthy life for all household members. Nationally, according to the USDA, nearly 15 percent of households are food insecure, meaning that they were without reliable access to a sufficient quantity of affordable, nutritious food at some point during the past year. When the study addresses vulnerable household members, they are referring to children and seniors. When it comes to those vulnerable household members, the Feeding America network is serving an estimated seven million seniors and roughly twelve million children, noting the actual number of children served being underrepresented due to the inability to conduct client interviews at child-only programs. Children are particularly vulnerable to the consequences of food insecurity because of the association between food insecurity, health, and cognitive development. It is alarming to learn that of Feeding America client households with children, nearly 89 percent classified as food insecure. Seniors can also face unique barriers to accessing nutritious food, such as decreased mobility, fixed incomes, health issues, or specific dietary needs associated with health status. Seventy-six percent of client households with seniors report facing food insecurity. The Feeding America client base represents a diversity of ages, ethnicities, races, and spoken languages. Clients face a variety of obstacles, including health, education level, housing, and employment instability, and insufficient income.

At a glance, identification of the Feeding America client base will tell you that 43 percent of clients identify as white, 26 percent as African American, and 20 percent as Latino. While minorities may make up a smaller share of the Feeding America client base, they are actually much more likely to receive assistance than their white non-Hispanic peers. More than one in four African Americans and one in six Latinos in the United States is served by the Feeding America network, compared to one in ten white non-Hispanics. Findings within this study also speak to the rise in diversity within households. Nearly a quarter of client households with at least one child are multiracial, which leans in the direction of indicating the growing diversity, particularly among the younger generations of clients.

For about 90 percent of Feeding America client households, the primary language spoken by adults at home is in fact English, although it is important to note that many clients indicated more than one primary language. The majority of the remaining clients use Spanish as their primary language, with .5 percent of clients indicating primary languages of Indo-European, Asian, Pacific Islander, or Arabic. It is important to note that the client survey was only offered in five languages (English, Spanish, Mandarin Chinese, Russian, and Vietnamese).

When it comes to the health of Feeding America's client population, nearly half report having poor or fair health, and a quarter report living with at least one household member in poor health, facing significant health challenges such as diabetes and high blood pressure. Facing poor health and food insecurity presents a multitude of challenges, including maintaining a healthy diet, which helps to manage disease. The Hunger in America survey was the first year of studies to include questions related to diet and disease. Results were alarming. In more than half of client households, at least one member has high blood pressure and a little over a quarter reported at least one household member to have diabetes. In households with seniors, the rates of both were notably higher. As with most health conditions and challenges, these likely increase expenses for the households that are already facing limited budgets, especially for individuals without any or sufficient health insurance. Even with those who are insured, medical debt can quickly accumulate with deductibles and uncovered services. More than half of client households reported having unpaid medical bills. And perhaps most upsetting is learning that almost two-thirds of households reported having to choose between buying food or paying for medicine and/or medical care in the past year, and a little over a quarter reported that they face this trade-off every single month.

Up until this point you have read a lot of statistics about the demographics of the client base served with food assistance by a leading nonprofit; some of that you already knew, some of that may have surprised you, and perhaps some of that you are still processing. The section to follow will help explain what the income and employment looks like for these households. Would you be surprised to learn that most Feeding America client households reside in stable housing? Although many clients did report experiencing recent housing transitions, the overwhelming majority (over 90 percent) of client households reside in nontemporary housing. To be clear, this means that housing is either stable or has the potential to be a long-term living situation. Clients most commonly reported living in houses, townhouses, or apartments. You may be the most surprised to learn that in fact over 25 percent of households living in nontemporary housing actually own their residence, some outright and some with a mortgage. It is only 7 percent of client households that reported living in temporary housing or housing unintended to be long-term, such as a shelter, motel, car, or on the street. Those households in temporary living situations tend to not have access to their own kitchen and are therefore much more common within meal programs than grocery programs. Many respondents did report making recent housing transitions, reflecting a level of housing instability. A little over 25 percent of clients reported living in two or more places in the past year, while a little over 15 percent of clients reported experiencing an eviction or foreclosure in the past five years. It is important to consider that some types of housing transitions may reflect clients' strategies for making ends meet. For example, 22 percent of those who participated in this study began living with another person or family in the past year.

Employment status is a critical factor that affects everyone's income and subsequent access to food. Many Feeding America client households struggle to secure adequate employment, which is a major contributing factor to their food insecurity. More than half of client households reported that at least one household member had been employed in the past year and at even higher rates for households with children at slightly over 70 percent, while only 34 percent of households with seniors reported to have at least one member employed within the past year. For one in three client households, the person that has worked the greatest number of months in the past year has in fact worked for pay more than six months. However, for over half of these households, the longest-employed person was only working part-time, which suggests limitations in the potential of how much he or she could earn. For many households, securing and maintaining employment is one of the greatest and most ongoing challenges. Factors including age and health status directly impact a household member's ability to seek and maintain employment. The reality for 46 percent of client households is that no household member is employed and reports to have at least one member who has sought work in the past four weeks as well as households where at least one member is unable to work due to a disability, poor health, or retirement. For many, the ability to secure and maintain adequate employment is directly related to his or her level of education.

When it comes to education, you may be surprised

to learn that many Feeding America clients are in fact educated beyond high school, with many adult clients reported as currently enrolled in schools. Slightly over 40 percent of households have at least one adult member with education beyond high school, including a business, trade, or technical license/certificate, some college, and those with two- or four-year college degrees. The most common level of educational attainment among adult clients is a high school diploma. But it is worth noting that some 20 percent of clients have also attended or graduated from college, and 10 percent of adult clients are currently students; that's two million who are full-time and one million who are part-time students. And just as we learned about the balance and tradeoff of competing financial responsibilities in the health and medical portion of this study, we see the challenge again for these households when it comes to education. Roughly 30 percent of households reported having to choose between paying for food and paying for education for a child or an adult each year.

We have started to build our informational foundation of who grocery programs are assisting. Another key component of this process is looking at the income of these households. Feeding America clients report living on lower incomes, the majority of which state that they live below the poverty line. The overwhelming majority of client households, however, reports surviving on minimal income. The median monthly household income among all households is $927, while the median annual household income is $9,175. Almost 75 percent of all client households are living in poverty with annual household incomes at or below the federal poverty level, which at the time of data collection was $15,510.00 for a family of two and $23,550.11 for a family of four. The federal poverty guidelines are used to determine eligibility for assistance programs such as SNAP (Supplemental Nutrition Assistance Program, also known as "food stamps") and WIC (Women, Infants and Children). Eligibility for federal nutrition assistance programs is contingent upon criteria such as household size, assets, citizenship status, and household income. A little over 80 percent of Feeding America client households fall at or below 130 percent of the federal poverty guidelines, which is the income threshold for SNAP eligibility. About 10 percent of client households recorded being between 130 and 185 percent of the poverty guidelines, making them ineligible for SNAP but eligible for WIC, The Emergency Food Assistance Program (TEFAP), or reduced price meals through the National School Lunch Program (NSLP) and the School Breakfast Program (SBP). The remaining client households reported incomes at 186 percent, or above the poverty guideline, making them unlikely to be eligible for any federal assistance, which leaves the charitable sector as one of the few sources of food assistance that they receive. It is imperative to note that some client households may appear income-eligible for federal assistance, however may have extenuating circumstances that preclude them from being eligible for federal nutrition programs again making the charitable sector the only source of food assistance.

For the first time in the history of this study, respondents were asked about US military service among members of their household, finding that 20 percent have at least one member who has served. Approximately 620,000 client households record having at least member who is currently serving either part- or full-time in the military, including service within the Armed Forces, Reserves, or National Guard. At the time of this survey, nationally, there were approximately 2.5 million military personnel. When compared to the number of Feeding America households that reported at least one person currently serving in the military with that approximate number of military personnel, the data suggest an estimated 25 percent of households with a member currently serving in the US military receive food assistance from the Feeding America network.

Client households frequently face difficult decisions in their pursuit to maintain food security. We know that Feeding America client households often survive on limited budgets and are confronted with choices between paying for food and paying for other necessities such as education and health care, as previously discussed. The dilemma continues for households that are often in the position of choosing between competing essentials associated with the cost of living. Over half of all client households report having to choose between paying for food and paying for utilities, transportation, medical care, or housing at some point during the year. One-third of households report making these spending trade-offs every single month of the year. These numbers are exactly why charitable food assistance programs are so vital. For households that have access to charitable food assistance, it is not just a safety net but an opportunity for clients to manage food expenses in a way that limited income can be distributed across a budget that provides for necessities such as rent and utilities. Although many households plan for monthly food assistance, it is reported that more than 37 percent wait until they have run out of food. In addition to accessing federal and charitable nutrition assistance programs and making the hard spending trade-off decisions, many households also use other coping strategies in order to provide for their families. The most common coping strategy for 79 percent of all client households is to purchase cheaper food, even if it's not the healthiest option. Unfortunately this strategy has known risks for negative health outcomes. For example, filling foods with little nutritional value that are high in fat, sodium, and sugar can lead to obesity, heart disease, diabetes, low energy levels, and poor overall health. Other coping strategies for securing enough food reported by client households included purchasing dented or damaged packages that were discounted, as well as watering down food or drink. More than half of all client households also reported receiving help from family and friends. And if all of that wasn't enough, 35 percent of clients reported selling personal property in order to purchase food for their household. One in five households reported success with growing food in a home or community garden as a coping strategy.

The difficult balance of spending trade-offs and the management of coping strategies that clients report facing on a regular basis highlights the very serious level of need nationwide. These strategies and choices also signal the need for a strong system of charitable food assistance that can combat the problem of hunger. It is rather clear that the general public is not aware of the scope of the problem or more would be done to eradicate hunger in a country where there is plenty of food for everyone. The information from this study should move you from ignorance to action! Connect with your local food bank and partner with them to ensure the readily available and abundant food supply is logistically positioned to be put in the hands of those who need it. No more thought, planning, strategy, or development beyond that is required. Simply go to your local food bank and tell them you are ready to help. They have the systems, the strategies, the supplies, and the surplus food ready to fight hunger and feed hope. Don't be ignorant; be informed, and be involved! Replace this missing piece to our pursuit of justice and turn the page to find out the final missing piece.

Are You Racist?

Here is the final missing piece to our pursuit of justice. You are probably a racist. As a pastor, people often ask me, "What is the church's response to racism?" Now I have some immediate reactions when I first hear that question. One of my first reactions is always, "Do you people not know the answer to this question already? Or I think, *What is wrong with you people? Are you people serious?* And then I realized that I have used the phrase "you people" so many times maybe I had some of my own problems that I need to work through. So we are going to work through them all together because it's a very serious issue in our culture and our churches. You can't turn on TV anymore without seeing something about racism on the news. It seems as if it's happening every week. I don't know why it's happening, and some of this is just going to be me operating as a casual observer of society trying to determine what is going on right now. I'm not sure what's going on, but we are seeing it a lot. Is it because it is happening more? Is it because the media are covering it more? Is it because there is this pent-up frustration that has never been handled as it should have been handled in times past? All those things at the same time? I'm not sure, but you can't deny this; it is a big problem that is part of our national conscience right now. So there appears to be a problem in America right now that we are dealing with at a pace and at a size that we haven't dealt with for over forty years. And before we go down the long road of what is wrong in America, why this is happening in America, I want to be clear about the fact that it is not just an American problem. Racism is a human race problem, not just an American problem. You can look all over the world, and there is racism all over the world. In the international community, they use a different word. They call it ethnic cleansing. All over the world right now you can find groups of people who are killing people who often are even in their same people group but are judged to be unnecessary or a burden. Even though they are the same race, the same color, because they are saying, and here is the evil of racism and ethnic cleansing, "I am better than you." That is the evil lie that drives it. In fact, one of the images that was burned into my brain twenty years ago is Rwanda. If you were not alive when it happened or you don't remember the story when it first came out, you've heard of it. No matter what your age, people remember what took place in Rwanda. In a hundred days, a little over three months, in a hundred days, over one million Rwandans were murdered. Racism? No, they were all the same color. Ethnic cleansing? Yes, different tribes. Because one tribe decided, and told the other tribe, we are better than you, and you don't deserve to live as a result of that. One million people dead because of an evil lie. There is racism in America; there is racism all over the world whether you call it racism or ethnic cleansing. Is there racism in the church? Only since the first day. So the first day is Acts chapter 2, right? You know the story. Everyone is so excited, they're joining the church; thousands of people are raising their hands. Going, "Oh, I love Jesus, this Jesus the Messiah who has come and was resurrected. I've heard His stories, I've heard Him talk, and I've seen His power. I want to be baptized in the name of the Father, the Son, and the Holy Spirit. Be filled with the Holy Spirit and move in power the way that Jesus and his disciples are moving. I want to join that church." That is chapter 2. In chapter 6, that's four chapters later, the Greek widows are saying from the back of the room, "Hey, how come all the Jewish widows are getting all the bread?" And the reason all the Jewish widows are getting all the bread and the Greek widows are not getting bread is because the

Greek widows are Greek. Now the disciples said, "Now wait a minute. We have to stop this right now." This is the church's first response to racism. You see the disciples had traveled with Jesus for three years; they saw his heart, and they heard the things that he said. They heard him say, "I have not come for people who are well. I am the great Physician; I have come for people who are sick." They saw the people that he healed and the people that he talked to. They had his heart, so they said, "We can't move on from here; we have to stop everything; everything stops right now." And they picked seven men to take care of this problem. And if you read the names of these seven men, these seven men are of different races and different ethnicities. Now they could have done what America has done in the past, and what the world is currently doing. They could have murdered all the Greek widows. They could have enslaved them; they could have ostracized them. They could have started telling jokes about how many Greek widows does it take to get a slice of bread. Now if you're laughing you have a problem, but we are going to work on that problem. They knew that this could not continue, so they stopped church; they picked some people to take care of it, and they moved on. But if you think about it, there is racism in America, there is racism in the world, and there is racism in the church, and the church doesn't seem to be as attentive to the issue as it was in the beginning. What is the church's response to racism? I believe the best teaching on the topic is in the book of John. The story of the Samaritan woman is the heart of Jesus on racism. I want you to know that John is my favorite book; there are so many chapters, so many verses in there that are so special to me. I like John 11:35. What's John 11:35 say? "Jesus wept." You people should know this because it's the shortest verse in the Bible. I can save your life if somebody said, "Oh, do you know anything about the Bible? Yeah, John 11:35: 'Jesus Wept.'" I love that passage because Jesus was about to raise Lazarus from the dead; he knew that there was no reason for him to cry. He was crying because everybody else was crying. Don't you want to serve a Savior like that? I love John 11:35; I love all of John. I love John because of the way John writes. Most scholars and theologians, agree that John would have written John in the later part of his life. Probably when he was eighty or maybe ninety years old. And it looks like what John did was take the other gospels, comparative gospels, sit down and read Matthew, Mark, and Luke. And here's what he did. He said, "Oh, you guys left out a story." This old man, John, he's reading what the disciples saw, what they were a part of, and he says, "Oh, you are not going to tell them the story about when Jesus washed our feet? You're not going tell that story. Oh, I'm telling that story." So he writes that story down. That is one of the fun things about how John writes; he was an old man, and old men say whatever they want to say! John says, "Oh, you guys aren't going to tell the story of when Jesus dragged our racially biased judgmental hearts into Samaria, and we had an encounter with "those people." None of you other guys are going to tell that story. Oh, I'm telling that story right now." So John goes through, and he tells stories that none of the other writers would tell. I feel like he's sort of telling on the other disciples because he was a part of the whole process, so I love John. So we are going to be in John chapter four looking at the story of the Samaritan woman, and I know you've heard the story before, and it's a story I can hear over and over again. I probably read it at least once every two weeks, and definitely once a month. This woman breaks my heart. And then she fills my heart with so much joy because she actually in a span of a few hours is able to fulfill the hope that she has had waiting inside of her for her entire life. Somebody should make a movie out of John 4, it's so fantastic. So we are going to start there because this is Jesus's response to racism. Let's start in John chapter 4, (John 4:1–6). One of my favorite verses in the Bible says he "had to go through Samaria." He did not have to go through Samaria. No, he didn't. All Jews who needed to go to Galilee would pass out of Judea across the Jordan River and

go outside of Samaria. If you need to see Grandma in
Galilee, you would head east, cross the Jordan River,
go around Samaria and back into Galilee. You didn't
go through Samaria. Here is why you didn't go
through Samaria. If you look at a map of ancient
Israel, you will see that Israel used to be a great nation.
It was one great nation, and then after Solomon, it
got divided into the northern and southern kingdoms.
And the northern kingdom was so wicked that God
had them hauled off by the Assyrians. The Assyrians
come in 722 BC; BC is going to be an important part
of the story here. In 722 BC they come and haul off
a lot of the Jews. And they take the Jews to another
country. And they replace the Jews they took out of
Galilee with people from other countries. Now the
Assyrians did this on purpose so that the races would
mix. So they would mix religions, mix cultures, mix
food, mix language, mix marriages, because they
would be so mixed up they couldn't form a revolt
against Assyria. So they did that on purpose. So the
Jews went away and married with people who came
from other places; they became Samaritans with
some semblance of a Jewish history. They believed in
the first five books of the Old Testament. They didn't
believe in the wisdom literature or the prophets. So
they had a little bit of Jew in them and a little bit of
four or five other countries that had moved in there.
And they became what the Jews would know as a

mixed breed. Dogs. Now a hundred years later or so, the Babylonians come, and they haul off all of Judea, the southern tribe, and they take them to Babylon. But the Jews who go into Babylonian captivity are very, very committed to serving God. They love him; they cry out to God, "Please save us; please redeem us; we're so sorry about what we've done. We want to repent." And God restores them, and they get to go back, some forty-three thousand go back the first time, and they get to go back and start to rebuild the wall. That's the story of Nehemiah. You've heard that story before. They all go back to Jerusalem, and they start to rebuild the wall and rebuild the temple, and everything is going to be fine, and the Samaritans are so excited that Jerusalem is going to be reconstructed again that they all come down and offer to help. And the Jews say, "No, no, no, you can't help. You can't help because you are a mixed breed. We don't have the same heritage anymore; we don't have the same religion anymore; we don't wear the same clothes anymore; we don't eat the same food anymore; we don't speak the same language anymore. Basically just let me make this plain for you, I am better than you." And from that day forward the Jews hated the Samaritans, and the Samaritans hated the Jews. So in about 30 AD, Jesus is walking through Samaria, "had to go through Samaria." No, he didn't. In fact nobody was going through Samaria. Only Jesus was going through Samaria. So 30 AD is where the BC becomes an important part of the story. From 722 BC to 30 AD, over seven hundred years these people had hated each other. Seven hundred years they would not go to each other's country; they would not talk to each other. They did not have a summit to sit down and work out all their differences; they did not work out a peace agreement; they did not negotiate with each other at all. Seven hundred years later, they still hate each other. And Jesus says, "We have to go through Samaria." Now Jesus said that, and we forget who Jesus was sometimes. I think we get caught up in the compassionate, loving Jesus, but you have to remember that Jesus was crazy. Crazy. We think about Jesus toward the end of his life, the end of his ministry where he focused on crying over Jerusalem. Promising to lay down his life for all mankind so that we could be reconciled with God again and be in relationship with God. And the healings he was doing, he was loving people, and we remember this loving, sweet, compassionate, gentle Jesus, and we forget in the beginning he was crazy. John chapter 4 is the first five or six months of his ministry. The first experience the disciples had with Jesus is that they all go to a wedding. They are following this Jesus guy now; they are not real sure who he is, what he is doing, or what he is all about, but they are following him. They go to a wedding, Jesus, Jesus's mom, and the boys. The guy runs out of wine; mom tells Jesus to handle it. Jesus says, "No wine? Watch this; wine for everybody." Jesus takes water and turns it into wine for a party!

And the guests say, "Man the wine now is better than before." So Jesus's first miracle, first little experience with the disciples, is him making wine for a party. The disciples are thinking, *Who is this guy?*

Just a few months later, their next experience with Jesus is going to be when they go to Passover in Jerusalem. They are following Jesus because he's doing all these amazing things, and he is crazy. They are following Jesus into the temple, but when they are following Jesus into the temple, guess what. Jesus is carrying a whip. You got twelve wide-eyed disciples following Jesus.

"What is he doing with the whip?"

Jesus kicks in the doors of the temple courts, starts kicking over tables, swinging his whip at people, and saying, "You people have turned this into a den of thieves. This is my father's house. You can't do that."

The disciples are going, "Oh man. What is happening? This guy is crazy!"

Jesus was a radical revolutionary restoring what God intended his relationship with people to be. So when Jesus turns to the boys with a whip in his hand and says, "Hey we are going to Samaria," they said, "Oh, yes sir, we are going to Samaria, we will follow you wherever you want to go sir."

So they go to Samaria. And when Jesus said he had to go to Samaria, he had to go to Samaria not because he couldn't get to Galilee any other way; he had to go to Samaria because it was time for him to break down the racial, ethnic cleansing, judgmental, "I am better than you" attitude that had permeated the entire society.

He says, "Here's what I am doing. I am taking you boys on a field trip for your first freedom march. We are going to march through Samaria against racism." So Jesus decides to take them to have an encounter with a culture they didn't know, a person they didn't know, food they didn't eat, a culture they didn't understand, and a language they didn't understand because he knows the way to break down racism is to have an encounter. Here is my prayer for you. I want you to know that I pray that God drags your judgmental, biased, racist heart to Samaria at some point in your life and that you have the encounter you need to have to understand where you really live in your heart and what needs to be done. Jesus was committed to changing people's hearts about people. I pray God takes you on the field trip you need to go on, the freedom march you need to walk in, to give you the encounter you need. The first step to breaking down racism in the church in America and all over the world, and the racism that may live in your heart, is to encounter people where they live.

But you can't just go "observe" people where they live like you go to the zoo and stand back at a distance and watch the wildlife in their natural habitat. You will need to engage the people you encounter. Let's read this next set of verses because this is what Jesus does (John 4:7–9.) I love these verses too. Remember these guys have never been to Samaria; they would never go to Samaria. Jesus has taken them to their first encounter; now He was going to teach them how to engage. Jesus says, "I am hungry; I want you to go down to that dirty little city, with those dirty little people, in this dirty little country, and get me something to eat."

And you can just hear the conversations go on in the disciples' heads. Peter is saying, "We can't go down there; we can't eat that food." Now they would have been eating the same food because the Samaritans believed in the first five books of the Old Testament, but it would have been prepared by Samaritan hands, and in their judgmental hearts there was no way they would have touched that food.

John is saying, "Someone should tell him, but I am not telling him. Have you seen him? He's crazy. I'm not telling him I am not going down there."

So they go down there to the city, and there's Peter standing at the falafel stand ordering falafels, and Peter is going, "Oh my God, they are touching my food. Do you people not have gloves to put on your hands? You are touching my food."

Jesus would be teaching the Samaritan woman, but he was teaching them first. It was part of the field trip; it was part of the encounter. The disciples get back from the field trip Jesus had sent them on so they could learn how to encounter and engage people, and they come back to find Jesus engaging with a Samaritan woman, and they are appalled. Now I don't have to go back and tell you why they didn't have dealings or engage with Samaritans; you understand that process.

The beautiful part of this passage is that it extends for another twenty verses. For another twenty verses this Samaritan woman, who's not supposed to be talked to or given any consideration at all, especially giving her immoral status, is engaged by Jesus, the son of the living God. For the next twenty verses, Jesus just talks to this woman.

Now here's what you need to understand about your own thought process. Pay attention to what Jesus does. Jesus just talks to this woman. Jesus will not agree with one thing that this woman believes. He will not agree with her sexual preference; she was having sex outside of marriage. He will not agree with her bible because her bible was missing some books as far as he was concerned. He would not agree with her theology because they are going to have a very clear conversation in a minute about where they should be worshiping. Jesus would not have agreed with one thing that this woman believed. But he still talked to her. He still engaged her because she was a human.

Now do you know why this lady is at the well at noon? Because she couldn't get water in her city. Jacob's well is half a mile outside of Sycar. Why isn't she going to the well in the morning and in the evening like everybody else does inside the city? Why in the heat of the day? And why not in her city? Well, because of who she was. She was an immoral woman, and when she went to the fountain in the morning in her city, all the other women would talk. She would hear the whispers. She would see the pointing. And all of them were saying this one thing: "I am better than you." She couldn't take that shame anymore, so every day at the heat of the day so she didn't have to see anybody, she carried a vase half a mile out of town, half a mile back into town because she was not accepted by anyone.

By his actions, Jesus said, "I do believe that you are a valuable person because you are a person." So they had this great conversation, and Jesus allowed this Samaritan woman to debate him about where they worship, what they do, who they are, and who the Jews think they are. It's a great engagement. We all need them.

So there is a client who comes to our food bank

who is covered in tattoos. And I am not talking about just the head tattoo or neck tattoo. I'm talking about every quarter inch of his face is covered in a tattoo. So one day I get a call from a panicked volunteer at our food bank, and the worker says, "Hey you better get down here. There is a scary-looking guy here."

So I go down there and see this tattooed guy standing in the line, and I go have an encounter because I have had a lot of encounters by now, and encounters don't bother me. I look forward to the encounters because they make me a better person. So I go up to the "scary" guy standing in line, and I ask him where he comes from and what he's doing. He tells me he just got out of prison in Utah; he is actually from Vacaville, and he is moving back to Vacaville trying to get his life back together again.

We talked about the tattoos. It's okay to talk about his tattoos. He knows he has tattoos. That is the part of your heart you need to work on. People know their circumstances. You don't have to not talk about stuff or avoid uncomfortable situations because you worry about what it is going to sound like or feel like. Jesus engaged; he talked about people's situations. So I engaged him as a person. I discover through conversation with him that he is homeless.

He doesn't come to the food bank for a while, so I start asking some of the other clients about him, and they tell me he is in the hospital. Based on his difficult outside living situation, he has contracted one of those superbugs—a horrible virus that put him in the hospital. The virus is so deadly that whenever I would go visit him in the hospital, I would have to put on those hazmat suits with the big masks and everything.

And I want you to know that this might be disappointing to you, but it is God's heart, and I want you to make this transition in your heart. When I am in the room with him, I am not talking to him about his eternal salvation. We had those conversations before, but I am not talking about those things now. I am not talking to him about his chronic homelessness. I am not talking to him about his substance abuse problems. I am just talking to him because he is a human being, a person.

We have had an encounter; now we have regular exchanges because that is what humans do who are not racist or concerned with ethnic cleansing or concerned about judging that you are better than somebody else, you engage.

Now I am going to politely apologize again and tell you that is what I'm praying for you. I am praying that God so wrecks you with the encounter he is going take you on, the field trip he is going to expose you to, that you begin to learn how to exchange with people that you don't understand or don't even agree with. You don't have to agree with people to be nice to people. Just exchange with them, and it will break down all kinds of walls that will allow you to be Jesus to people in difficult circumstances the way Jesus was Jesus to the Samaritan woman.

But you don't just want to exchange; you also want to encourage. That is what Jesus says. Encounter them, engage them, and encourage them. Here is a verse where Jesus encourages her (John 4:25–30). This is a woman who doesn't talk to anybody in town and can't be seen with people in town. She leaves her vase after her exchange with Jesus and goes down into the town. She is so full of hope that she is not afraid to go into town and say, "Hey everyone, look, I know who I am. I know what you think about me, but I have met the Messiah." She leaves her vase because she is in a hurry and because she knows she is coming back.

Now I want you to pay really close attention in context to what actually happens in this passage. What does Jesus actually do for this woman? Jesus does nothing for this woman. He doesn't heal her. He doesn't wave his arm and say, "May all your sins be forgiven and you be released into a new life; you be baptized in the power of the Holy Spirit, and you will live in power and in harmony with God." Jesus does nothing for this woman but remind her of the hope that she already has inside of her. By encountering her and engaging her, he reminded her that she had once had hope in her life. That she had once believed that her life could be different. He reminded her that she believed there is a Messiah, a savior. She believed there was potential and there was a possibility that her life could change. All she needed was for someone to encounter her, not avoid her; engage her, not dismiss her; and encourage her, not judge her. That is all she needed to be released into the life that God had for her.

If that was the plan of the living son of God, that is all you have to do for people as well. You are not responsible for fixing people's problems. You are not responsible for saving people. You are responsible for living out the hope that lives in your life so that people see hope so that it reminds them of the hope that lives inside of them. And you can't do that if you don't encounter them, exchange with them, and encourage them.

I have told you a couple of stories about people from our food bank. Let me end with one more. You want to be encouraged? You should come to the food bank someday. Hundreds of people will be standing around waiting to get food. Now when you get to the food bank, you won't see people gathered in their own little groups of color, ethnicity, or any other demographic. You won't see it. They encounter, engage, and encourage each other because they have realized that they are not better than everybody else; they are everybody else. So they encourage each other every day.

There is an elderly gentleman with a trach tube sticking three inches out of his throat. He shows up every day with watches he has purchased at garage sales that don't work; then he goes home, repairs them with the little money that he has, and brings them to the food bank and gives them away to anybody who is there, regardless of race, ethnicity, demographics—makes no difference to him. He is just trying to encourage people.

I am telling you, you just need to encourage people. You are not responsible for fixing everything. Encounter, engage, and encourage. Do you know that for some people, you will be the only God they ever see? You are not going to be able to drag them to church; they may not read your Bible, but they are looking for someone who is not afraid to encounter them, engage them, and encourage them so they see the hope of God living in you that reminds them of the hope they have in them. That is what sent the woman running down the hill.

Encounter people; I'm praying that it happens to you. Keep looking over your shoulder because it is coming. You engage that person when you have that encounter. And then don't worry about fixing all of their problems; just encourage them in a way that you would like to be encouraged. Here is one sentence that will sum up the entire chapter:

For God's sake, people, just be nice!

PART II

Seeing Your City

This section is designed for lead pastors and church planters. In the next few chapters I will be writing from the vantage point of the team leader and the one responsible to vanguard the vision, set the pace and make the key decisions to move the church and organization forward. This content will also be useful for all leaders who aspire to build churches for the glory of God that are making a real impact in their cities.

How do you see your city? Many pastors and church planters develop an unhealthy "love-hate-relationship" with their city. The common perspective, that is evidenced by the continual conversations at conferences and leadership gatherings can have tones of a martyr complex when it comes to the cities God has called us to pastor. This prevailing attitude and perspective is revealed through a variety of statements and paradigms that sound something like this: "it's a hard place", "it's known as the church graveyard", "we are the most unchurched city in…." "people don't attend church in our city, there's too many other options" "our city council and city leaders are anti-church", "our region is the seat of Satanism and occult activity" and on and on it goes. I've often wondered how many international headquarters Satan can actually have. I do not say this with any tone of rebuke or condescending attitude because I too am guilty of pointing out all the flaws of my city and complaining how the city leaders, planning commission and maybe even the Russians have been involved in a conspiracy to thwart the growth and plans of our church. If you have fallen to this subtle mindset and trap, in this section I want to invite you to see, speak and pray for your city in a different way. Here has been a key verse that I have adopted regarding the small-town God has called me to pastor, perhaps you could use it as well.

> "LORD, *you alone are my inheritance, my cup of blessing. You guard all that is mine.*
> **The land you have given me is a pleasant land.** *What a wonderful inheritance!*"
> Psalm 16:5-6 (NLT)

You are Called to Pastor a City

Pastors are gatekeepers. They are God-appointed spiritual leaders that are gifts to cities and regions, not to buildings and memberships. When I begin to see myself as a pastor of my city, not a church within my city, I will think differently, pray differently and envision the church that God sees. A church that is large, influential, creative, prosperous, showing up in every realm of education and city expansion, a church that cannot be ignored. My pastor, Wendell Smith, used to make this statement from the platform, which I have adopted and made my own; *"everyone needs a home church, and everyone needs pastor and I would be honored to be yours"*. He believed it, lived it and when he would say it, you actually wanted to say "yes! Sign me up". When we realize we are called to pastor the city, see people that are not inside the church yet as on their way, realize that we are a big deal to God, the church is the hope of the world and that God has "counted us faithful, putting us into the ministry" (1 Timothy 1:12) we will walk in new authority with new expectations and vision. Ask God to help you see yourself as the pastor of a city, a region, of people that have never thought about attending a church service.

Pray for Prosperity

For I know the plans I have for you," declares the LORD, "plans to prosper you and not to harm you, plans to give you hope and a future.
Jeremiah 29:11(NIV)

That is one of the most quoted, prophesied, painted, embroidered, embossed and famous verses in Christendom, second only to John 3:16. And rightfully so, it's an amazing promise that truly reveals the heart of our Father for his people. I love the fact that this verse and promise was given to people who found themselves in self-imposed exile. That God so loves us and is looking down the road that even while we are headed into in a place of bondage, barrenness and self-inflicted suffering he is already making a plan to lead us out. (seventy years in advance) What a God! Yet I believe that Jeremiah 29:11 is inseparable from the context and principles we find just a few verses prior.

"Also, seek the peace and prosperity of the city to which I have carried you into exile. Pray to the LORD for it, because if it prospers, you too will prosper."
Jeremiah 29:7 (NIV)

Now while it might be a stretch to call the city where God has led you "exile", there are some similarities we should consider. We are temporary residence on a broken planet that have been called to bring a heavenly kingdom into our current location and situation. What I want you to see and embrace from this verse is God's instruction to "seek the prosperity of the city". This is a potential game-changer for churches and leaders. Instead of seeking the prosperity and peace of our church, we are to take responsibility for, intercede for and be active in producing the prosperity of our city. Therein lie the key to our growth, influence and continual momentum. When we take ownership of the prosperity of our city, which starts with the most unprosperous portions and neighborhoods, then "we too will prosper." Then we can quote and believe verse 11 with great confidence… "Plans to prosper you, plans of a hope and future"

Seeing Who Jesus Sees

The toughest thing for the religious community of Jesus's day, to wrap their heads around, was the fact that he didn't come for the people who had it all together (by their own standards). He not only came for those outside the faith community, but he surprised everyone by coming for those that nobody thought would ever be invited into 'the green room of faith'. Don't you love that about Jesus? Always bringing the blind guy, the leper, the prostitute, the rip off artist, the notorious sinners, the mafia bosses and drug dealers of his day into the inner circle. This is not a once or twice random occurrence but such a consistent pattern in the life and ministry of Jesus that it cannot be ignored. Jesus loves and welcomes messed up, broken people that society has long overlooked and developed a "program" for.

> *"Go quickly into the streets and alleys of the town and invite the poor, the crippled, the blind, and the lame.' After the servant had done this, he reported, 'There is still room for more.' So his master said, 'Go out into the country lanes and behind the hedges and urge anyone you find to come, so that the house will be full. For none of those I first invited will get even the smallest taste of my banquet.'"*
> Luke 14:22-24

I think the main lesson we can learn from Jesus dinner guest selection process, is that Jesus sees people differently than we do. We see the woman at the well for the embarrassment and immoral person she has become while Jesus sees a precious daughter and the evangelist for a city. We see Zacchaeus as the despised IRS agent that he was while Jesus sees a lonely man who is looking for real change and will be a future leader. Now you may disagree a bit with my assessment of how we see people but that is because you know the rest of these familiar stories. But how about the unwritten stories that walk the streets of your city? Every homeless person, gang member and immoral partier that mocks what we give our lives for. Do we see them through eyes of grace and with their redemptive potential in mind? I think at times I do, but not nearly enough or clearly enough. Oh, to see people like Jesus, to love people like Jesus and to honor those who are living a life without honor. I think if we could, we would prepare a large table and invite an eclectic list of guests, and that's what this book is really about.

The Road of Favor

You might agree that there are two general aspects of favor in the life of a believer. One is the result of relationship and the other a bi-product of our activity. Relationally we are "saved by grace through faith" *(Ephesians 2:8-9)*

We understand the grace that saved us to be best defined as "unmerited favor", that is, God's undeserved influence on our hearts that created his likeness and reflection in our lives. This is the mystery of salvation and the essence of the gospel. Thank God for grace! The favor I want to discuss in this chapter is **the favor that can be realized by pastors and local churches who are willing to walk the road of favor.**

I never wanted to plant an average church for nominal Christians. I never had a vision for survival or status quo. And I don't think you do either. Ever since we were 8 people meeting in a living room praying big prayers and dreaming God-sized dreams I've always longed to be a part of something that God was breathing on, heaven was smiling on, momentum was pushing on and I was simply trying to stay on the surfboard and ride the waves of God's gracious momentum, we call it favor. Can you relate?

Of course, that has not always been our reality, but I must say after 21 years of fighting this good fight, 1,000+ battles, a million people problems, hundreds of series preached through and far too many egg casseroles in the green room later, I'm still longing to ride the waves of God's favor and move with the currents of His Grace. So, here's a couple things you already know yet I'll remind you again.

In order to travel the road of favor:

- **Find out what God has placed his favor on and get involved in it**
- **Determine what he has already graced and make it your priority**
- **Discover where the "burden of the Lord" has been placed and get under it**
- **Identify what he is already blessing and partner with him in it**

This is where many churches and leaders get off track. We want the favor we see resting on great churches and leaders, so we are duped into thinking that if we have all the ways and means of the "successful church" then we will have the favor and influence they enjoy. When in fact most established ministries that we would aspire to be like: I.e. Hillsong, Elevation Church, Gateway Church, Life Church, Church of the Highlands, and the list goes on, are not large and influential because of what you now see on a weekend service or conference. That's simply some of the fruit of favor, not the root. If you came to our main campus on a weekend you would see some of the same features; great sound system, amazing band, lots of people, LED screens and of course, a plethora of moving lights (my personal favorite). But those amenities that we now enjoy neither produced nor have the power to sustain momentum, they simply facilitate the river of God that flows in our community. That river of favor, presence, growth and prosperity finds it's impetus in the same place that it did when we were 75 people meeting in a rented elementary school, or 500 meeting in a community center, or 4,000 meeting in a shopping center… it's the simplicity of reaching those that others have overlooked! That's right, that's the secret recipe of momentum and favor right there. Ready? **Simply reach, love, invest, restore and champion the lives that nobody else cares about and you will be amazed at how God will keep broadening the road beneath you and opening doors that no man can shut.**

Here's how it works:

When Jesus started His ministry by picking up Isaiah's scroll, he prophetically read about himself and fulfilled a prophecy that was written some 750 years before his ministry debut. As he stood to read the weekly portion of the Torah, he looked out at a small gathering of Jews in the synagogue in Nazareth, and read: Luke 4:18-20 (NIV)

"The Spirit of the Lord is on me, because he has anointed me to proclaim good news to the poor. He has sent me to proclaim freedom for the prisoners and recovery of sight for the blind, to set the oppressed free, to proclaim the year of the Lord's favor."

This is a very familiar passage for all of us, but I just need to point out these 5 powerful words: *"He as anointed me to....."*

The anointing is toward something, it's to do some specific exploits. The "divine enablement" was upon Jesus for a specific task and I would submit that the reason for the anointing, or the empowerment has never changed. Favor comes to those who will embrace the "Jesus job description". Fast forward to the end of Jesus ministry and he looks at his disciples after His resurrection and says:

> *"As the father has sent me, this is how I am*
> *sending you", Then he breathed on them*
> *and said, "Receive the Holy Spirit"*
> John 20:21-22

The anointing can best be defined as: *divine enablement, God dwelling in us and resting on us to accomplish what we could never do on our own.* If we look at the anointing that rested on Jesus and the purpose for the power, we can begin to see a pattern throughout the life and ministry of Jesus that will illuminate the road of favor. Let's revisit the words of Isaiah that Jesus fulfilled and embodied. He said "the Spirit of the Lord is upon me to….

- Bring good news to poor people
- Bring freedom to prisoners
- Give sight to the blind (spiritually and physically)
- Bring freedom to oppressed people
- Declare a time of favor (to those who are without)

If we were to do an extensive study in the ministry style and patterns of Jesus we would see over and over again that the grace, the momentum, the favor and the anointing he carried were for the purpose of reaching the least, the broken, the poor, the hungry, the sick, the forgotten and the non-religious. Here's another soundbite.

Jesus answered them, "Healthy people don't need a doctor—sick people do. I have come to call not those who think they are righteous, but those who know they are sinners"
Luke 5:31

So, my simple thesis for this chapter is this: **The anointing is for a purpose, and that purpose is to reach the same target audience that Jesus was empowered to reach**. Now, the gospel is for everyone and yes, the rich and influential people need a savior as well, no doubt. But we miss a key element when we overlook the obvious ministry road that Jesus paved for us. This ministry road of favor has on-ramps that look like: feeding the poor, developing prison ministries, helping single moms, targeting low-income and poverty areas of our city with resources and tangible love and making a place at the table for those who are convinced they don't belong.

Jesus gives us a clear invitation to journey on his road to favor. On that road there is guaranteed momentum, resources, power and divine enablement for the leaders and churches who will dare to be a church for "the least of these". Yes, it gets messy, it's not quick, slick or on sale, but I wouldn't want to travel any other ministry highway than the one Jesus paved for us.

What's in Your Hand?

"What's in your hand?" That question comes from a conversation that God had with Moses when God called him to lead at a level that Moses was convinced was above his paygrade and beyond his gift mix. This is not an uncommon conversation and scenario with leaders: we wait in the desert until we think we've missed our window. God shows up and gives us new marching orders in a season we were not expecting him. We give excuses why it won't work or why he should find a better suited candidate. God reminds us that It's never been about our qualifications but our availability and off we go in faith to change the world. One detail of this story that I find intriguing, is the fact that the very object that identified his failure in one season, becomes the symbol of his victory in the next. Think about it. Moses was an up and coming ruler in Egypt until he snaps one day and becomes a wanted felon. On the back side of the desert for forty years, he comes to grips with the failure that is his life, his mortality and the fact that he will probably die tending goats in the desert, not a glamourous or motivational life but he had come to grips with it. So in a very real way, holding that staff in his hand represented his long-formed identity that caused this potential deliver of a nation to settle for goats in the desert. But GOD! Think of the poetic beauty that the very rod that identified his life of disillusionment and failure becomes the very instrument he raises over the waters of the Red Sea to lead God's people to freedom and fulfill his life's calling. Only God! Well, I digress but it's a great preaching point and I think there are some leaders reading this chapter who are holding the rod of failure and disappointment while God has been planning an epic comeback. That's just who He is and what He will do with you!

Back to the question at hand, What's in your hand? When it comes to taking on the needs of our broken communities and the overwhelming weight of fighting against poverty, hunger, gang violence, sex trades and human trafficking in our cities, we can quickly conclude that we really don't have what it's going to take to make a dent in the problem, so "why get all worked up about it?" When in reality, the mustard seeds of generosity and benevolence that you and your church are holding have the power to release the kingdom into your city in a way that will astound you.

Humble Beginnings

There is a line of scripture from Zechariah that is often quoted to church planters in an attempt to encourage them, although I'm not convinced that's the net result. "Do not despise small beginnings". I remember people quoting that to me when our church started, and I remember not only despising the small beginning we were struggling through, but I despised them quoting the verse. I'm much more mature now. I would like to take a look at this verse again, in context, and in light of making a huge impact in our communities.

Do not despise these small beginnings (the days of small beginnings), for the LORD rejoices to see the work begin, to see the plumb line in Zerubbabel's hand."
Zechariah 4:10

Get this visual. Zerubbabel has been sent by God himself to rebuild the temple in Jerusalem after it's complete destruction. After a long journey, he's staggers into this city of ashes, broken down walls, piles of rubble and only memories of former glory. Yet God sees him. The searching eyes of the Father are upon him while Zerub walks through the garbage heaps with a plumb line in his hand. Now we do not use plumb line's anymore in construction, we use lasers and sophisticated instruments to determine what is plumb and level. But back in the day the plumb line was a simple instrument by which they would lay the cornerstone perfectly level and square to the future structure. And it says, "God rejoiced to see the plumb line in Zerubbabel's hand". God delights, celebrates and gets excited about a guy with a string in his hand!? Why? God could already see the finish product, the worship, celebration and life of a nation rebuilt. So, it is with your city and what might seem like a truly insignificant attempt to make an impact. God rejoices at the long-range results of what we can only dream about now.

Currently we are serving 90 blocks in 3 counties. Every week we see over 200 volunteers serving our communities. Ever month we are feeding over 25,000 people and the scope of what God is doing continues to multiply exponentially as we open new campuses and plant new churches in other cities…. But it didn't start like this. It didn't look anything like this. We started our "Adopt-A-block" ministry with 3 people taking on one block, knocking on 20 doors and simply asking if there was any way we could pray for them, serve them or help them with their groceries this month. But let's back it up even further. When our church was just 6 months old Thanksgiving was arriving and I decided we were going to feed as many families as possible with a full turkey dinner. So, I had our church community bring their frozen turkeys, along with all the extras, to my house where we would organize, strategize and deploy the patron saints of turkey into the needy neighborhoods of our city. I still remember the entire floor of my garage and driveway filled with boxes of food and 118 frozen turkeys. Sure enough, we went door to door, into the worst of neighborhoods and gave away those 118 turkeys. Since that first thanksgiving we have been able, by God's grace, to give away millions of dollars of food and resources and work with some of the largest food distribution organizations in our nation. We did not see all that coming, but God did.

So get busy with what you have now. Start a program, start a block, take on a school project, be creative, find out where the need is and do your best to meet it, launch something that is sustainable and watch God help you grow it. What is in your hand? What do you have access to right now that would be a blessing and an answered prayer to people in the under resourced neighborhoods of your city? Never make excuses based on what you do not have to give away or get caught in the trap of waiting until you think you're ready and resourced enough to make a difference, because you might never get started.

What is your plumb line? Get it out, take a walk, hold it up and with eyes of faith see some messed up neighborhoods rebuilt for the Glory of God. Who knows, maybe you'll hear the laughter of your heavenly Father as He rejoices over the future impact you will make. As I look back I'm pretty sure he was celebrating those 118 turkeys in my driveway.

Getting Unstuck

Pastoring and leading a local church now for several decades, I have seen a pattern in the life and times of our church, as well as the churches and pastors that I have the honor to network with and help along the way, and here it is. From time to time, we get stuck. Yes, great churches, with big vision, growth tracks, prayer ministries, discipleship and training programs and the latest-greatest social media game still get stuck. This usually occurs after a season of momentum or a successful run of implementing fresh vision and then it hits. For no apparent reason and no known sin in the camp, no overt demonic attack or church split that is threatening our existence. Just a slowing of momentum and what was once exciting is now predictable, yesterdays 'new and improved' becomes todays 'we've done that, and we're bored' and without realizing it, great church plants and healthy churches can find themselves in maintenance mode. As a visionary and a leader, I quickly break out in a rash (metaphorically speaking) when I sense the organization is slowing to a crawl, or even worse, getting stuck with no signs of change. So here is my thesis for getting unstuck; **In every season in the life of a church, God entrust his leaders with keys that will open new doors and unlock new arenas of opportunity.** Our job as leaders is simply to seek those keys, recognize when they appear and then use them in a timely fashion, more on that later in the chapter. Right now, let's consider what Jesus said about keys.

> *"And that's not all. You will have complete and free access to God's kingdom, keys to open any and every door: no more barriers between heaven and earth, earth and heaven. A yes on earth is yes in heaven. A no on earth is no in heaven."*
> Matthew 16:19 (Message)

Traditionally, we understand this verse and concept of "binding and losing" as a component of prayer and making declarations, but perhaps there's more to it in regard to being given "the keys" of authority and change for our cities. Here's a definition that will help the discussion.

A KEY:

A unique implement that opens a unique or specific door or secured area. Without the right key, the area, the room or the supply remains unavailable or unattainable

With that said, I would ask you to consider a couple things; a. what keys have you accessed and used to get you where you are today with your church or organization? B. what unused keys are waiting to be discovered and turned in order to open some new doors and arenas for your future?

I believe that **"keys" are an entrustment to God's leaders** but they must me valued and stewarded well in order for new keys to be issued and entrusted. So, a few things about leadership keys.

1. **Keys are personal**: that is, they are unique to your journey, your city, the size and age of your church and what is needed right now to get unstuck and see the kingdom advance in your setting

2. **Keys are seasonal; This** means they must be used before their expiration date. We are familiar with the two primary Greek words for time in the New Testament; *Chronos* and *Kairos*. Kairos means "the window of time" or

"the season of God's favor", "the favorable and acceptable time"

3. **Keys are sequential:** The door you move through now positions you for the next, and the one after that.

4. **Keys are hidden:** this means we must pursue God, seek the keys for the next season and depend on the Holy Spirit to reveal what we cannot figure out.

5. **Keys are useless until activated:** let's not just go to seminars and conferences and become professional key collectors and polishers. Once we have identified the key for our future we must initiate some things, make some investments and necessary changes.

6. **Keys represent new authority that is inseparable from new responsibility;** We'd all like to see our influence double or triple, our churches grow exponentially and our ministries make an impact in ways that we have only dreamt about. Yet many leaders are discouraged in the process of taking new ground when the reality of taking on new responsibility and financial investments becomes inevitable. New authority is always accompanied by new responsibility.

7. **God delights in giving us the keys**

The reason I presented this concept of keys and doors and getting stuck is that I truly believe community outreach, City impact and providing for hurting people in our areas of influence is a key that we cannot afford to pass by or leave unturned. When we pick up this key and begin to use it we will see doors open in our cities with people and places we never dreamed we could access. This has been our experience as we have invested well and been faithful with the keys that God has given us for our city.

A Story of Getting Unstuck

For years our church had been doing some "part time benevolence"; An occasional project, always presents at Christmas and turkeys at Thanksgiving. We had a small food pantry and feeding program and although it wasn't massive it was a consistent part of our budget and our hearts were good. Our church had been in a growth mode for several years and we found ourselves holding the title as "the largest church in our county". The problem was, we were not carrying an appropriate burden and responsibility for hurting people, given the size of our church community and the resources we were being entrusted with. For several months, I could not put my finger on it, but momentum was waning, numbers were flat lining, even the feel of the services was changing and the number of salvations were diminishing. This perplexed and troubled me. We were doing the stuff! the sermons were as good as ever, the band was cranking out the worship tunes and the machinery was well oiled... yet our great friend, momentum, had quietly left the building. During this season, I was scheduled to travel to Tokyo for a conference and while I was there I found myself in a consistent prayer mode for our church and the mystery of "stuck". One day during the conference God graciously spoke to me in sentence form, this was one of the clearest moments I've had in my ministry journey and it was a moment where God handed me a key. Now disclaimer, before I tell you what I heard I want to preface it by saying, hearing from God in sentence form is subjective and everyone has their own personal pneumatology, but for me... this was God, and this was undeniable. The Holy Spirit spoke this exact sentence to me: *"I've called you to care for your city and If you don't go home and take responsibility for the hurting and under resourced people in your community, The Father's House will become progressively irrelevant"* BOOM! This was a wakeup call, a sledgehammer in the spirit, the blinding light on the road... all the above. I went home, met with our board and we got busy. We bought a Good-year tire store and invested $1.3M turning it into a distribution center for food and resources for our county. We brought Pastor Raymond on staff to oversee all that was City Impact and started learning everything we could from L.A. Dream Center, in regard to infiltrating our neighborhoods for the glory of God. This was really the birth of WE LOVE OUR CITY - "The Community Outreach Ministries of The Father's House". By God's grace I picked up the key in Tokyo that day, initiated some big-time change in our organization and started down a road of favor and influence that we have never regretted or looked back from.

Now I'm not saying that opening a benevolence center is your key, for this season of your journey. Maybe it's hiring an administrator or investing in a new sound system, maybe it's implementing a GROW track or rethinking your small group ministries. But here's what I do know. If we want to see the church gain and maintain consistent momentum it will require picking up and turning the keys of loving our cities in a tangible way. Our motive must be love, not bigger ministries and budgets. Our goal is to help those who cannot or will not help themselves at a particular stage in their life journey. As we invest our time and resources to love people beyond the walls of our churches, God is busy doing something beyond us, he is moving our boundaries, increasing our influence and enlarging our heart for the people we have decided to reach and serve. It's a thing of beauty! #unstuck

The Imagination of Ministry

"Necessity is the mother of invention"
Unknown author

While Jesus was teaching on the shores of galilee a crowd of twenty thousand plus gathered to hear him teach and to receive all the miracles and wisdom he had to give. (see **Mark 6:30-44**) Yes, this is the famous story of the five loaves and two fishes, and I just want to point out two statements that Jesus made to his team during this miraculous event. First, when the disciples suggested sending the massive crowd into local villages for dinner, Jesus responded with *"you feed them"* to which the disciples were obviously caught off guard and had not remotely considered this as an option. When they presented the factual impossibilities of Jesus' suggestion, He ask them this follow up question; *"how much bread do you have?"*

This is actually a consistent pattern when God is

getting ready to do a miracle, he sees what we have to contribute in order to release faith and be a part of the answer. Consider miracles like the widow's oil, Moses staff, or the disciples letting their nets down on the other side. And this is the key to reaching our cities, stepping into the provisions that only faith can release and using our imaginations to consider new possibilities in solving big problems. God was not asking the disciples to produce the miracle of multiplication or logistically solve the predicament, he simply wanted them to get involved with whatever they had and watch him work. When the need far exceeds our resources and the demand is so great we don't even know where to start, it's time for some faith-fueled imagination.

We have seen this principle and pattern at work many times as we have expanded our community outreach. The need always exceeds the supply and our seemingly insignificant contributions appear to be a small drop in a large bucket. Yet when we take simple steps of faith, in response to the real needs of people, God consistently gets involved and adds His super to our natural.

This happened recently in a ministry that has now grown into an amazing outreach for under resourced kids in our city. The name of the ministry is Kicks 4 Kids and the way it was birthed was a combination of divine inspiration and local imagination. I'll let James tell the story:

"We were just serving with a We Love Our City team, assisting with an elementary school's after school program when the seed idea for Kicks 4 Kids was birthed. There was a young boy playing basketball with a couple of our volunteers. I remember just watching them play, and I happened to look at the kid's shoes. The shoes were these grey imitation Converses. The shoes were so small for his feet that the shoelaces had exploded apart, and the tongue of the shoe was bulging out the top. For some reason, I took a picture of his feet. A few days later I began to look at the picture of those shoes, and I had a feeling there might just be a way to meet that need. After some prayer and brainstorming we thought, 'mmm I wonder if local sporting stores and businesses would get involved if we shared our vision?' and sure enough, the idea took off and soon we found our teams carrying hundreds of pairs of brand new, donated shoes into all the neighborhoods where we serve through adopt-a-block. This was the launch of Kicks 4 Kids. To see their smiles, watch them play ball with their new shoes and visibly put on a new sense of worth and joy is more than I could have ever ask for. and it all started with a need and a 'what if?'"

"For me, K4K was just the beginning. I have ideas for giving kids, that are uninsured or under insured,

free eye exams and prescription glasses. I have had this vision of a mobile business center/GED school set up in an RV. This mobile business center would be remodeled to have desks, computers, printers, and free Internet access. It would go into lower income areas to give people access to technology so that they could complete their GED, search/ apply for jobs, and print resumes. I have an idea on how to help people enter the housing market through small micro-loans funded by the Small Business Administration, through a nonprofit organization. I just believe that if we will dare to believe and create some new programs that God will show us how to do it and provide the resources"
James Burns (We Love Our City Volunteer)

Now the analyst and the critic could quickly come up with 20 reasons why those ideas would fall apart, have already been attempted or would not be a sustainable model. But that's not the point, is it? There's never a shortage of critics, skeptics and analyst to tell you why your idea won't work. What we need is people of simple faith and obedience that are driven by the needs of people and a desire to do whatever it takes to bring them some practical help. James and Amanda get it.

This is how effective ministry happens; you go, you see the need and let the need move you to a solution. I believe many of the programs and effective ways to reach people with the tangible love of God have yet to be imagined or developed.

Multiplication of Workers

As a church planter, lead pastor and visionary I am forever studying, analyzing and theorizing on why churches grow or don't, impact a city or do not, thrive or spend all their time and energy just trying to survive. And although church building and City transformation can be a complex subject here's my simple theory: **Churches grow, plateau or decline in direct proportion to the new people that are being equipped and released to do the ministries they are passionate about**. You probably don't need chapter and verse to back up that statement but here's a couple just in case;

When he (Jesus) saw the crowds, he had compassion on them, because they were harassed and helpless, like sheep without a shepherd. Then he said to his disciples, "The harvest is plentiful but the workers are few. Ask the Lord of the harvest, therefore, to send out workers into his harvest field."
Matthew 9:36-38
So Christ himself gave the apostles, the prophets, the evangelists, the pastors and teachers, to equip his people for works of service, so that the body

> *of Christ may be built up until we all reach*
> *unity in the faith and in the knowledge of the*
> *Son of God and become mature, attaining to*
> *the whole measure of the fullness of Christ.*
> Ephesians 4:11-13

Paul goes onto tell us that when the equipping, releasing and serving takes place that the body will grow up, be recognized as Jesus on the earth and continue to be "healthy and growing and full of love". Now that is the kind of church that we all want to be a part of and the kind of church that will impact a city.

So, here's the wrap up and big take away from this chapter. Not everyone is going to be a "platform person" a small group leader or gifted to teach and preach. Very few will feel the call to 5-fold or full-time ministry and there's only so many people you want on the worship team. But everyone can find an effective and fulfilling place of serving people if we will release them to use their imagination and see what God is saying to them. This creates passion, ownership and a high level of excitement when their vision becomes reality. The direct and indirect result of loving our city continues to fuel the passion and momentum of our church, enabling us to grow and reach more people with the message of grace. Imagine the possibilities!

The Long Game

Here's a tip: Give your strategy a decade and your vision the rest of your life! We've all heard the statement "my overnight success was twenty years in the making". It's so true. Ministries and churches that are making a difference and shaping culture in their cities, have probably been at it for quite some time. That doesn't necessarily mean that old churches are effective or new church plants are ineffective, it is simply the reality that city transformation is not a quick and easy process. We have currently been serving our city for 21 years and I would say that the real momentum and exponential growth has occurred in the last 5-7. "The long game" is not talking about driving your golf ball but developing a long-term strategy that you are committed to implement, support and diligently work out.

Allow me to remind you about a principle in the word that we need to directly apply to serving our cities. In Genesis 8:22 (NIV) God makes this promise to Noah and all humanity:

> *"As long as the earth endures, seedtime*
> *and harvest...will never cease"*
> Jesus goes into a bit more detail
> in Mark 4:26-29 (NLT)

> *"The Kingdom of God is like a farmer who*
> *scatters seed on the ground. Night and day, while*
> *he's asleep or awake, the seed sprouts and grows,*
> *but he does not understand how it happens. The*
> *earth produces the crops on its own. First a leaf*
> *blade pushes through, then the heads of wheat*
> *are formed, and finally the grain ripens.*

We understand the agricultural and spiritual realities of these words, yet how often do we hesitate to plant the necessary seed and patiently tend the ground as we await the results.

Another way to apply the truth of seedtime and harvest is to have a ministry mindset of **seed + time = harvest**. The hardest gap in the life of faith is the gap between the promise and the fulfillment, the vision and the fruition, the seed planting and harvest time, yet this is a reality that remains "as long as the earth endures". So, I would encourage you to get busy planting and tending and if you've been planting and tending, don't be weary in the waiting. God will bring a return in your ministry and in your city. Your coming harvest is as sure as the promises he has made in His word.

After about a decade of serving our city we began to see a noticeable shift in the spirituality and hunger for God in our city leaders. Some of those "long-game results" have included our previous mayor coming to our church to receive a check for a community program, then coming back for another visit and eventually giving his life to Jesus on an Easter Sunday morning. After his conversion, it was not uncommon to see him on the front row, early service, every Sunday. He has recently gone to be with Jesus, what an honor to introduce him. Currently the City Manager, Vice- Mayor, City Council members, Chief of Police, large numbers of City Police, County Sheriffs and fire fighters attend regularly. This is all the direct and indirect fruit of serving the hurting people in our community and building a reputation of a church that truly loves their city. Our goal was never to see if we could draw the influential people of our city in order to open doors and work with us, but there is a spiritual reality at work here, that when we consistently care for the impoverished and the broken, God will bring the well-resourced and influential as well. This is new testament stuff, Zacchaeus is gonna show up at the same dinner with the ex-leper, the blind guy and woman at the well. This is the kind of church we want to build and the kind of influence that is available when we commit to sowing the seeds of benevolence over the long haul.

One final verse:

The same One who has put seed into the hands of the sower and brought bread to fill our stomachs will provide and multiply the resources you invest and produce an abundant harvest from your righteous actions.
2 Corinthians 9:10 (VOICE)

What seeds do you have in your possession right now? What "righteous actions" are waiting to be initiated in your community? think of the resources that God is just waiting to multiply and the harvest of souls and influence He has intended for His church! Remember; "He gives more seed to the sower", not to the dreamer or the preacher. What do you say we sow the tangible love of Jesus into our cities and keep doing it until our race is run? I believe this is a key that God will use to open doors in our cities that are currently shut. This is a non-negotiable if we are going to build churches that impact cities and cause us to be a shining light, a city on a hill, and a church that cannot be ignored. Let's go love our cities.

PART III

WE LOVE
OUR CITY
AND WILL TAKE
RESPONSIBILITY
FOR IT.

WHO WE ARE

We Love Our City is a service-driven nonprofit organization that exists to identify and resolve poverty related injustices on the local level. Our mission is to provide services that address immediate needs while creating lasting solutions to social injustice. We have a range of community specific outreaches where we focus on:

- RELIEF
- RESTORATION
- RELATIONSHIP

JOIN THE TEAM

Behind every outreach you will find the heart that inspires vision and the mission that propels action. We are committed to connecting resources to the under-resourced. The more help each outreach has, the further out we can reach. Our hope is that this guide will help every person find his or her place in the grand calling that is caring for one another and loving our city together.

OUTREACH PROGRAMS

ADOPT A BLOCK

The heart of Adopt A Block is to create an atmosphere of change in our community by adopting underserved neighborhoods and the individuals and families who live in these areas. The mission for this outreach is to find a need and fill it. We go to the adopted blocks every Saturday to bring groceries, clean up trash, remove graffiti and provide activities for children.

ADOPT A SCHOOL

The heart of Adopt A School is to extend resources to the youth of our community in order to encourage a healthy lifestyle and learning environment. The mission of Adopt A School is to partner with local elementary schools to provide assistance with food, programs, and special events. We also supply backpacks filled with supplies and deliver fresh produce to students on a weekly basis.

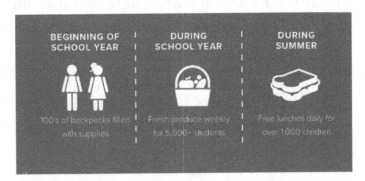

BEGINNING OF SCHOOL YEAR	DURING SCHOOL YEAR	DURING SUMMER
100's of backpacks filled with supplies	Fresh produce weekly for 5,000+ students	Free lunches daily for over 1,000 children

ADOPT A BUILDING

The heart of Adopt A Building is to build relationships with residents in one of the most under-resourced areas of San Francisco by adopting a building and the individuals and families who live there. We serve alongside San Francisco's City Impact in the Tenderloin District. The mission of this outreach is, every floor, every door, every month to provide food, care and compassion to the tenants.

THE STOREHOUSE

The heart of The Storehouse is the belief that hunger is something that no one in our community should endure and access to food is fundamental to the well-being of a strong and vibrant community. The mission is to provide free food and personal care items to all who are in need. The Storehouse believes in fighting hunger and feeding hope.

COMMUNITY GARDEN

The heart of the Community Garden is to improve quality of life by establishing an oasis for residents to come together and engage in community building and overall health. The mission of this outreach is to provide a space to grow fresh produce that will in turn supplement family grocery budgets, promote healthy diets, and create opportunities for exercise, education, and interaction.

BOOKMOBILE

The heart of the Bookmobile is to instill the love of reading within all children. The mission of the Bookmobile is to offer mobile library services to connect children and their families to the resources they need for their educational, recreational, and lifelong learning needs. We partner with local school districts and public libraries to redistribute books from their inventory.

AFTER SCHOOL PROGRAM

The heart of the After School Program is to create an encouraging environment for children to continue learning when class is over. The mission of this outreach is to help the children in our community thrive and provide a safe environment every weekday where students are offered homework assistance, literacy guidance, team-building activities, leadership development, and exposure to the arts.

GRAFFITI REMOVAL

The heart of Graffiti Removal is to beautify the neighborhoods, communities and cities where we live. The mission is to work with the local fire and police departments to remove gang related graffiti and tags as quickly as possible. Partnering with local government is vital as graffiti is known to lower property values and can incite criminal activity.

MOBILE HAIR SALON

The heart of the Mobile Hair Salon is to bring beauty, confidence and personal care to school age children in our Adopt A Block neighborhoods. The mission of this outreach is to provide haircuts, hairstyles, manicures, and personal care products to under resourced children. The Mobile Hair Salon operates on the volunteer efforts of licensed cosmetologist and donations of equipment and supplies.

MOBILE MEDICAL CLINIC

The heart of the Mobile Medical Clinic is to see our community thrive in vibrant health. The mission of this outreach is to bring wellness checks, blood pressure screenings, diabetes education, and a variety of other services to our Adopt A Block neighborhoods. The Mobile Medical Clinic operates on the volunteer efforts of registered nurses, medical doctors and donations of medical supplies.

MOBILE DENTAL CLINIC

The heart of the Mobile Dental Clinic to bring smiles and health to our community. The mission of the Mobile Dental Clinic is to provide routine dental checks, basic dental essentials and education on oral health to adults and children in our Adopt A Block neighborhoods. The Mobile Dental Clinic operates on the volunteer efforts of registered Dentists, Dental Assistants and donations of dental supplies.

MOBILE VISION CLINIC

The heart of the Mobile Vision Clinic to provide our community with vision screenings to ensure that they get to see their loved ones and our community thrive. The mission of the Mobile Vision Clinic is to provide vision checks, eye care and education to families in our Adopt A Block neighborhoods. The Mobile Vision Clinic operates on the volunteer efforts of registered Optometrists and Nurses.

THE THRIFT HOUSE

The heart of The Thrift House is to support The Vacaville, Napa and East Bay Storehouses that provide food to over 20,000 people a month and to provide emergency clothing to those in need in our community. The mission of The Thrift House is to be able to give more to more people in our community. The Thrift House operates through volunteer hours and community donations.

KICKS FOR KIDS

The heart of Kicks for Kids is to equip kids with shoes that fit to give them confidence, dignity and the ability learn and play. The mission of Kicks for Kids is to provide brand new shoes to children in our Adopt A Block neighborhoods. Kicks for Kids operates on volunteer efforts, monetary donations and partnerships with local businesses such as Reebok, Fleet Feet, and Genentech.

PROJECT NEW DAY

The heart of Project New Day is to provide our homeless neighbors with a path back to the workforce. The mission of Project New Day is to gain purpose, work skills and the means of purchasing needed food, clothing, and other necessities through gift cards to local businesses for those who participate. We partner with The Vacaville Police Department's Community Response Unit to make this possible.

JUVENILE OFFENDER DIVERSION PROGRAM

The heart of the Juvenile Offender Diversion Program is to give juvenile offenders a second chance to reverse negative trends and be healthy, productive members of the community. The mission of this program is to provide community service opportunities in an attempt to divert youthful offenders from the juvenile justice system. As a part of the program they serve the community through our outreaches.

PRISON OUTREACH

The heart of the Prison Outreach is to establish relationships with incarcerated men and women to assist in their transition back into society. The mission of this outreach is to challenge, change and improve the lives of the inmates in the program through relationship and programs. Examples of available programs include, anger management, writing skills, money management and community reentry guidance.

COMMUNITY OUTREACH INTERNS

The heart of the summer internship program is to provide participants the opportunity to gain perspective into the role of community leadership through service-oriented programs and outreaches. The mission is for the interns to gain experience in non-profit management while navigating the complexities of government-funded resources.

we ♥
our
city

🐦 @weheartourcity
📘 We Heart Our City
📷 @weheartourcity
#weloveourcity

Printed in the United States
By Bookmasters